Who is a Christian?

OTHER COMPASS BOOKS

★

Apologetics and the Biblical Christ
AVERY DULLES, S.J.

Bishops: Their Status and Function
KARL RAHNER, S.J.

Christian Revelation and World Religions
JOSEPH NEUNER, S.J. (Ed.)

The Church is Different
ROBERT ADOLFS, O.S.A.

The Desecration of Christ
RICHARD EGENTER

The Grave of God
ROBERT ADOLFS, O.S.A.

Images of Authority
J. M. CAMERON

Light on the Natural Law
ILLTUD EVANS, O.P. (Ed.)

Man and Wife in Scripture
PIERRE GRELOT

Man at Play, or, Did you ever practise Eutrapelia?
HUGO RAHNER, S.J.

Mary's Place in the Church
RENÉ LAURENTIN

The Mass and the People of God
J. D. CRICHTON (Ed.)

The Ministry of the Word
PAULINUS MILNER, O.P. (Ed.)

Mutations of Western Christianity
ALBERT MIRGELER

Obedience in the Church
ALOIS MÜLLER

Prayer as a Political Problem
JEAN DANIÉLOU, S.J.

Primitive Christian Symbols
JEAN DANIÉLOU, S.J.

The Variety of Catholic Attitudes
THEODORE WESTOW

Who is a Christian?

by HANS URS VON BALTHASAR

Translated by JOHN CUMMING

COMPASS BOOKS

LONDON · BURNS & OATES

BURNS & OATES LIMITED
25 Ashley Place, London S.W.1

First published in Great Britain 1968

This is a translation of Wer ist ein Christ?
(Benziger Verlag, 1965).

Nihil obstat : MICHAEL ASHDOWNE, S.T.D., PH.L., Censor.

Imprimatur : ✠ PATRICK CASEY, Vicar-General.
  Westminster : 21 December 1967

Unless otherwise stated biblical quotations
are from *The Revised Standard Version of the
Bible,* copyrighted 1946 and 1952.

Made and printed in Great Britain by
Northumberland Press Limited, Gateshead
Set in Linotype Pilgrim

Contents

Contents

I

A Preliminary Skirmish

AWKWARD QUESTIONS

YOUNG people nowadays ask awkward questions. They want the lowdown. But before they ask their questions they take a look at things as they are. No wonder they're suspicious. They've every reason. The people they look to for an answer claim to be Christians; but what do these so-called Christians base their title on? On convention, tradition, or something drummed into them in the classroom? But just a minute, what are *they* based on—your tradition, catechism and going-to-the-sacraments? On the Gospels, you say. But if you read the New Testament you get a very different picture of things. So you settle on an intermediary: the teaching authority of Holy Mother Church. Then it all gets rather difficult. You can't just turn round and point straight back to the beginning of it all. Instead you have to peep round corners and re-enter what is, frankly, a labyrinth. That's the way it starts: the familiar and, let's admit it, tiresome argument about the rights and claims of the appointed ministers of God: that they know Christ's exact intentions and have the authority to interpret what he said, and then press their interpretations on the consciences of other men.

But somehow or other these explanations—and you can hardly blame them for that—always bear the mark of their own times: sooner or later those who accept them

7

have to face up to the realization that new times and new ideas tend to reduce the force of interpretations that were once pronounced so very emphatically. Now they seem pale, conventional and often embarrassing formulas. Some obviously have to be rejected as part of the irrelevant ideology of the past. An *aggiornamento* is unavoidable. Some people are loud in their praise of the Church's continual "power of renewal"; others—though less vociferously—are disturbed when positions that have been maintained so doggedly, and for so long, are—like insignificant outer defences or obsolete fortifications—condemned, evacuated and razed to the ground. Then comes the question (even more awkward now): What's your standard for making all these decisions? The sands of history slip through the anxious scrutineer's fingers; our thoughts turn to the beginning—the concrete basis of it all. But where's that to be found? Where can we get an unequivocal answer to the question: "Who is a Christian?"

Even if it's a question that doesn't cause me any personal anguish, I can't escape other people asking me. If I'm a father, then my son wants to know. I can't very well pretend I know the answer—I can't in all conscience deceive my own son. If I'm a teacher then I abuse my authority if I sell children down the line with ideas for which I certainly wouldn't hang from a meat hook.

If I'm sitting in the canteen with the others at work, or having a drink, I can't parry the awkward questions as easily as the teacher in the schoolroom. Friend or foe will soon find out what sort of assurance I can give. If I don't ask myself, others will certainly force me to.

PAINFUL ISOLATION

And so the Christian is in a more isolated position than

ever before: he asks questions as well as being asked them. Until now there was always a point of contact for religious discussion; at least there seemed to be some kind of common basis to rely on; and only differences of secondary importance needed debate. St Paul's situation in the Areopagus after a morning stroll through the temples and shrines of Athens seems almost enviable. His companions are "very religious men": they not only see Divinity ruling throughout the universe, they even have no difficulty in believing—with more or less certainty—in a number of individual revelations and recognize the State cults. It's just a question of revealing the "unknown God" and then showing the difference between his manifestation in the death and resurrection of Christ and the imperfect perceptions of the other cults. Of course, for a time there's a tough struggle with Rome, but victory comes relatively quickly. From then on, through the Middle Ages, Renaissance, Counter-Reformation, Enlightenment and Idealism, until the last century, religious controversy remains within the framework of the debate in the Areopagus. St Thomas Aquinas debates with the Jews and the "heathen" (i.e., with Islam): a basic acknowledgement of the Divine and the distinction between Deity and world forms the common ground of discussion; the individuality of God and his revelation through one or more historical prophets are also accepted by both sides. These are the basic premises for the conciliatory and often very accommodating theological disputations of Roger Bacon, Ramón Lull and Nicholas of Cusa.

The Renaissance continues this tendency by returning to classical antiquity and, on the basis of a gradual discovery of certain facts about the history of religion, by seeing Christianity as the highest and perfect expression of the religious faculty in man; an examination of the competitors' claims reveals the absolute superiority of the revelation of Jesus. The Enlightenment shares basically the same view, even though the stress shifts and world religions now appear wholly as part of the religious "equipment" of mankind as such. But this equipment, being one of the possibilities or "faculties" of man, is subjected to increasingly precise philosophical and then historico-scientific analysis: if man "can" be religious, then he can also compare his God with himself. Then it's possible to show how the various images of God correspond to man's changing needs and various stages in his civilization; how, once he's come of age, he can be brought to see that he manufactures his idols for his own ends: to satisfy his need for love and adoration, his sense of justice, and his longing for a happy life after death.

That kind of doll's house is no longer suitable for men who have come of age. They can get along without it; in fact, they can get along quite well.

Once man reduces things to his own size he seems to get ahead much more quickly and more purposefully. Nowadays no reasonable man says his prayers, for the age of contemplation is past: we live in the age of action. Man is in sole control of himself as well as his world; and he makes what he wants of himself. What about you? I know you're a Christian, but aren't you ready to get into step with this new pulsating rhythm of man in control of himself? You're not! Then you've decided in advance against the logic of world history; you're not just taking the risk of being run over: you're already underneath the wheels. In the past, for pagan philosophers as for Christians, everything was directed to the "conversion" (turning, *epistrophe*) of the world to God. Today everyone (and that

10

means you too, you who have looked to God for so long
—too long) is asked to make a major turnabout: conversion to the world.[1] Perhaps this doesn't seem to fit your
Christian sense of logic. Well, didn't the founder of your
religion send his first disciples out into the world? Surely
you contradict yourself if you're the only one to be looking back when everyone else looks ahead.

The Christian looks about him for some advice—for
assistance. What he always thought was a secure protective wrapping of good comfort has fallen away. It's painful to be stripped of your shell; it's embarrassing to find
you look like some fossil from the long-buried strata of the
past.

ETHICS AND STATISTICS

As religion declines the form of ethics that was based on
religion disappears spontaneously. On the one hand we
have an ethics based wholly or largely on the concept of
eternal justice and reward. But man is either moral in
terms of his human condition, or else morality doesn't
come into it at all. A transaction made on the basis of
punishment or reward is morally dubious; it certainly
implies the absence of any form of free personal choice. On
the other hand we have the higher morality where that
which is good is done in imitation of the highest good:
because God gives us life and unselfishly causes his sun
to shine on the good and evil alike, we try to show our
gratitude by being unselfish ourselves. But what if God
didn't make us? Then unselfishness would just be part of
human nature. Isn't this evident in the social world of
animals, an arrangement which among men becomes only
a higher form of self-control? Isn't this so-called selfless-

ness merely a function of man's natural impulse towards self-expression—a kind of self-love and instinctive desire for self-preservation found among sub-human creatures in a quite elementary form? Then morality should come somewhere near the mid-point between self-concern and altruism—to the right of it in fact. Man certainly doesn't need to invoke God, and it's ridiculous to think he needs a personal revelation in order to see what's obvious.

Aren't the excessive moral demands of Christianity far removed from the actual state of things in this world? Like the ethics of the old, long-vanished world, they posit a morality for "heroes" (you call them "saints"), for aristocrats better than ourselves—like the high-minded protagonists of the Greek tragedy, who must be kings, gods or heroes (similar to the martyrs or heroic saints, or even angels of the Christian theatre); whereas the common people appeared on stage only in bawdy comedies, where men and gods duped one another quite happily. So it was long ago; and so it was throughout the Christian centuries —for far too long a time.

The actual nature of man and his possibilities really become clear only if we refuse to ignore him in favour of such highflown patterns and ideals, which are unattainable for the average man and which no one could possibly hope to achieve. We must see human nature as it really is. The easiest way to do this is to look at questionnaires, reports and statistics. The average obtained from a fairly widespread sample shows that most people belong to a common mass with its own quite satisfactory form of civility and something approaching a hierarchy of values: you certainly don't need to impose one from outside (or, rather, from above). If you take people on their own terms you'll undoubtedly get a better reception than if you come down to them with ten or even five commandments from some lofty mountain accessible only to the élite.

Christians, too, are material for the statistician, since a certain percentage of mankind consists of Christians. And a fraction of that percentage is (even more nominally) Catholic. But it's anyone's guess what form of programming would be needed for a proficient survey of the number who are "really" Christians and Catholics. I've no idea what method you could use to find that out.

But don't statistics allow us to determine precise, generally valid and therefore binding standards of human behaviour—the sort of norms that would provide, say, a police force with a positive, universally applicable basis for action? There's no need for all the fuss about an *a priori* categorical imperative, or an equally aprioristic natural law. Surely it's enough to say that a man, if he's to live with his fellow humans as a biological yet reasonable creature, must obey certain definite rules of the game and temper his instincts to some extent. What else? Yes, of course he should be liberal and tolerant as well. As long as they are not entirely incompatible with the general good, different religions and moral systems can remain open to the free choice of the individual; and free competition of this kind should in the long run be to the advantage of all the recruiting bodies. It's already a lot to be a good man; no religion dispenses with that requirement: the best recommendation of any religion in the eyes of mankind as a whole is that it produces honest citizens—good men. And good men are those who actually behave in what most people recognize as the right way to live; for most people retain an image of good behaviour they like to find as a reality in others, even if perhaps they can't manage to live that way themselves.

THE BURDEN OF THE DEAD

Unfortunately other people know something of the long history of Christendom. They've got a better memory for it than the Christian himself, for he wants to make a new start and be as up to date as his peers. The burden of tradition weighs on other people only slightly or not at all : the dead had their responsibilities and we've got ours. Whatever they got up to when they were alive doesn't concern us. Even Protestants hardly feel the weight of the first fifteen centuries of Christianity. But the Catholic can't just shrug off all this history : the Catholic principle of Tradition (note the capital T) reminds him that the very Church he belongs to has done or allowed to be done things that we certainly can't approve of nowadays. Of course it can all be put down to evolution—the inevitable process of men learning how to grow up; but what a tangle of secular and sacred we get into when we try to think that one out. Anyway, it's clear that the Christian is part of the tangle : he receives the tradition and with it his share of responsibility, whether he likes it or not.

Since this is the state of affairs, perhaps the honest reaction is not only an immediate recognition of sinful responsibility but also a full one that will emphasize the harsh tragedy of the past. Things that were not only permissible but even recommended under medieval popes seem, from the double perspective of Christ's own word and our present state of knowledge, absolutely impermissible and even gravely sinful. They were obviously diametrically opposed to the spirit and word of Jesus. Forcible baptisms, inquisitions and *auto-da-fés*, St Bartholomew massacres, the conquest of new worlds with fire and sword as if the release of brutal exploitation were also the way of the religion of the cross and of love; unasked for and utterly absurd meddling in problems of developing natural science; proscriptions and excommunications by a spiritual authority which behaves as if it were political, and even demands recognition as such. This seemingly unending register of crime and corruption is a shameful inheritance to come into when the errors are so conspicuous, so unmistakable.

It's humiliating; but it's unfair to throw stones when no one is alive to stand up and plead justification. We have to recognize that Christ is the news of God's absolute claim on men—one that goes beyond the absolute claim of Yahweh on his people of times long past; that, whatever the means, something of this call to men is handed on in the irreversible choice of the apostles and the Church; and that the administration of this authority by sinful or short-sighted men can bring about incalculable harm that would otherwise have been avoided. The connection of the contemporary Christian with those who are dead saddles him with a reckoning for past errors which he has to be able to bear, not just unwillingly but patiently and, in secret, even thankfully. Does any man know how *he* would have behaved had he lived in the ninth or fourteenth century?

It is consoling for the Christian who must bear this bitter load to realize that evil is remembered more easily than the Christian things in the world that are good but aren't apparent or impinge only indirectly on the general consciousness. Who counts and weighs the hidden acts of unselfishness by which evil is prevented, the acts of selfless atonement and charity, and the significance of prayer? Who apart from God really knows the experience of saints who have been through heaven and hell; who affect—obscurely—whole tracts of history; who move mountains of guilt and show the way out of countless dark moments? All this must be mentioned in passing, if only to emphasize that until these hidden assets are taken into account the debit sheet for the Church can't be made final.

The bitter burden can also press on the contemporary Church, trying so hard to free itself from unnecessary bonds. But it must be a slow process if, in every aspect of its being, the Church is to become the living reality already revealed to individuals for so long a time. If structures which have been called in question are torn down comparatively quickly, it doesn't necessarily mean that they will be replaced by any desire for vision, understanding and realization of a positive and constructive alternative. The most questionable and yet most firmly established of these structures is undoubtedly infant baptism—an early "decision" with incalculable results. It can certainly be justified, but not as the only possible solution. The Christian advantages of the other solution are also undeniable if considerable—and the highest possible—sacrifice and loss are taken into account. The anticipation of a proud and unrepeatable lifelong decision for God in a condition where the consciousness and conscience are as yet unformed; then the gradual development of reason and the formation of an ability to make for oneself a decision that's already been made, which can finally be ratified seriously, superficially, or not at all. A real paradox: a real problem. And it's all the more a problem today when popular traditions and the sociological security of a Christian community are disappearing or have for the most part already vanished. Yet infant baptism is just part of the burden we bear.

TWILIGHT OF THE IMAGES

To people who live without God the voices of Christian culture and civilization say nothing about God, or at least say it so faintly that it can't be heard. The Western world owes the inspiration and construction of its most beautiful works of art to the spirit of religion. This is just as true of the works of classical antiquity which, in general and individually, arose from veneration of the divine, as of all the original creations of the Christian centuries. No one has yet been able to show that great and valid works of art can be produced on an irreligious basis. As Goethe remarked to Riemer: "Men are productive as poets and artists only as long as they're religious; otherwise they become merely imitative and repetitive: as we are in relation to classical times, whose greatest works were all artefacts of faith which we reproduce only as quaint or romantic fancies." Euripides' *Iphigenia* was the dramatic presentation of an almost insane obedience to the gods; Schiller's translation[2] simply cuts the theological conclusion and therefore the whole root of the play; even Goethe's own version[3] is no more than the schematized reflection of a noble humanity.

If we ask what Christian architecture, literature and music, produced for God and intended to tell men about God, have to say to a contemporary spectator, reader or listener, the answer is in every case: Not what they were designed to say. "But in every note I can hear the message of. . . ." Rubbish! He doesn't hear it at all, he just puts it on tape and switches it on and off. All this can be very discouraging for the Christian: it leads him to question the communicative power and therefore value of works of art other than those of the present day; it can bring him to doubt or dismiss the value of any ideology or sophisticated form of expression: "Surely all that stuff is pointless nowadays?" or "Well, as far as we're concerned today, it's just one big embarrassing fiasco." What has the admittedly elegant poise of a Roman basilica got to do with Christianity? It's not much different from the secular market hall of the time. And what connection can you find between a fortified Romanesque church and the Jesus Christ who told his companion to put up his sword? And what has the blustering heavenwards drive of the Gothic cathedral to do with the kingdom of heaven within us? And what (if, in embarrassment and perplexity, we just miss out the Renaissance) have the elegant convolutions of the baroque style to do with the bare wood of the cross? Some people are glad that since then Christianity hasn't put on the same kind of show—it's better, so they say, to have nothing at all than all that. A Christian is ashamed of Christianity's past when he sees it through the eyes of a "modern". (The hordes who rush across Europe, surging blindly from one monument to another, don't help to balance the account: indeed, such termites are visible signs of the decay of Christianity).

But the Christian need not be ashamed. He must distinguish faith from the outward expression of faith. For faith *can* be everlasting; but the phenomena that stand as the works of faith are bound by time. And these works are themselves spurs to new and greater faith. Even a baroque saint frozen in perpetual ecstasy, her eyes raised for ever in adoration, is a question asked of you: What's the equivalent for *you*? Have *you* so surrendered yourself to

God that you can imagine an equivalent and vital expression of your self-giving? Have you, with your mental snigger at the traditional analogy between musical harmony and perfect harmony, even half the soul needed to reflect the purity of a work by Palestrina or Haydn? Come off it. Don't play that game—the bored dissenter who sees nothing when he has the eyes of faith to see with. Don't give in to untenable theories or seek support from boneless ideologies. Remember that you're also free to say Yes, when you find an easy denial on the tip of your tongue. Realize that you're free to make use—full use —of what you already have as well as to try what is new.

Precisely because you have been made free in Christ Jesus and don't have to clutch at any earthly thing, recognize the freedom of your active fellow Christians and behind them that of all the devout and godly men and women who like you declared their faith in God and the works that are of God. Don't be taken in by the facile writing off of everything that was Christian in the past as having nothing to do with the things of this world. That would be to ignore its love of phenomena and knowledge of their innermost workings—a love and intimacy far beyond those apparent today. Perhaps you're seriously persuaded that the petty abstract schematizations of today are closer to this world, more faithful to its real nature, more concrete than the achievements of the great Christians? Who really has a deeper knowledge of human nature: Villon, Chaucer, Langland, Donne, Blake and Grimmelshausen—or the unfeeling pornographers of today? Leave the latter to themselves and don't be taken in by Christians who tell you that only the stark realism of our contemporaries has revealed man in the full gravity and sinfulness of his existential situation, without the frills of pagan idealism.[4]

And don't be dismayed if no one goes for the genuine goods any longer. "I know how to live when things are difficult and I know how to live when things are prosperous. . . . I am ready for anything through the strength of the one who lives within me," says Paul (Phil. 4. 12-13). The Christian must be able to live through the sunsets around him; but he must never allow his own sun to be obscured. He may share the poverty of his (spiritually) poor brothers but he may not renounce his birthright— the very one that has produced all the riches they have sold and lost for their mess of pottage. Undoubtedly as the lights go out he will be enclosed in the darkness—darkness over the earth. But to be wrapped in night is not to share the spirit of night; that the Christian must never do, least of all out of an alleged sympathy with others: "Do all that you have to do . . . so that you may be God's children, blameless, sincere and wholesome, living in a warped and diseased world, and shining there like lights in a dark place" (Phil. 2. 15).[3a]

THE AVERAGE AND THE UNIMAGINED

A Christian shining like a light? But how? The same kind of difficulty we started off with. Everyone feels that it just isn't like that any more. It just won't do. Now everyone can see himself and his Church from the outside, the way the ordinary man sees it all. It hits you suddenly when you look at things that way. It's as if you've been trotting into the same old church for Mass for years and years without noticing anything wrong. But one day a renovations expert points out the multitude of cracks, and the crumbling masonry and shabby fittings you've been blind to. "Got to pull the whole thing down," he says. "Well, it's either that—a demolition job—or a piece of pretty thorough reconstruction work." You have to look closely at it then. If the whole lot could come down on your head any day, you don't just sit there smug and satisfied; if you've any sense you give a hand in the rebuilding at once —go as far as your own strength, ability and time allow. Fright's a good persuader; there's nothing like fear of one's personal safety to give the "courage" needed for an *aggiornamento*. Right, we'll get rid of all those mouldering stone frills, nineteenth-century ironwork—only gather dust and put people off. Might as well redesign the interior while we're about it. What we want is a neat, unornamented place in the modern style. After all, it costs less when you get down to figures. A thorough renovation makes you feel quite up to date: it's curious, but taking things apart gives you a satisfying feeling that you're being constructive.

Any rebuilding of the Christian structure demands a close examination of the basic design: some kind of return to the starting point. Take down the Counter-Reformation plasterwork, uncover the evidence of the Reformation. Let's begin to understand how the building came to be as it is with all its essential buttresses and its accretions. Perhaps we'll even get down to the foundations and find the plain gospel of Jesus Christ.

We've done quite well to get to the point of dissatisfaction with what's gone before; to discover that outsiders were justified in finding us untrustworthy witnesses. If we look at statistics—and that's the resort of every pundit who's asked for a definition—then the "average Christian" turns out to be—frankly—a vague and elusive creature. On the sidelines we find those whose Christianity centres on a baptismal certificate, Christian marriage and burial, and perhaps First Communion and Confirmation for the kids. Then there's the crowd of Easter communicants—shading off into the company of Sunday massgoers, to be distinguished further by such true marks as no meat on Fridays, reading Catholic newspapers, or even covenanted offerings. Here we begin to meet with the stalwart figure, the G.C., or "good Catholic". His double, the "good citizen", always does what the traffic lights tell him to do. Well, the "good Catholic" keeps a look-out for the warning lights of the Ten Commandments: of course, it's the sixth that glares most fearsomely, that's the one to look out for first, whereas the fifth, seventh and eighth impinge not so much as orders straight from God as things that a "good bloke" does only when he's pushed—really in a jam. Of course we have to take social status and cultural background into consideration: in some country districts regular church-going can count as a matter of principle—as much as a personal or family feud that's held to tenaciously until the grave. It can be a matter of principle too, to be a real man and live in a kind of honourable neutral territory between the parish priest's viewpoint and one's own opinion: "Let's be fair and square about it. You know your job and I know mine."

But we've forgotten the so-called "zealous" Christians up there on the heights. We've got to count them in. After all, it's the average we're after. They're the ones who try to live a genuine Christian married life, make real individual prayer an indispensable part of their lives; really love their neighbours by actively caring about them—doing something about the grindingly poor, the neglected, aged, forgotten and helpless; who really care about the Church as a missionary Church; who—if they're priests—live their

22

entire lives in holy orders, not just by performing the set rites but by following Jesus and living in poverty, chastity and obedience.

Those who take a risk and face the searching light bear the brunt of the investigation. They are the structural components that will receive the most raps, knocks and taps to see if the material is really sound; to see perhaps if there isn't a suspiciously hollow response from this or that supposedly firm support—or pillar of the establishment. The question "Who is a Christian?" isn't addressed to the first-mentioned group with quite the same force; with a certain degree of humility they refer us to the "practising" or full-time Christians, especially when they themselves are not fully convinced of the value of specialist knowledge and activity. When you're a declared believer, being tapped for essential hollowness is a pretty delicate business: here's the real test whether you're a Christian. Here's where we have to make a detailed analysis and fill in the test-card.

Firstly: who is entitled and in a position to *decide empirically* who is a Christian? For example, can a non-Christian ask the questions? Is it possible to find out at all, and what standards do we use?

Secondly: who is entitled and in a position to decide by reference to certain norms of behaviour what a Christian really is? And what standards, requirements and regulations are to be put before those who have to answer? It's not at all straightforward when you really get down to it. So it's not irrelevant to ask:

Thirdly: the existential question: can a Christian himself really determine if he is a Christian? If he says he is, can he show that what he says is true?

The question "Who is a Christian?" is inescapably bound

up with all the attempts at reform within the Church to-day—yet it's largely ignored. I say *ignored* because, on the one hand, people behave as if they already know all the answers and, given their secure basis of proven knowledge, have only to enforce certain *preventive* measures. *Ignored* because, on the other hand, the freedom is assumed radically to question the traditional answers and guidelines: so that past norms are examined and found wanting on the basis of criteria that have been accepted without any test of their validity. It's not difficult to make out these criteria that are taken for granted: they're easily seen in the main tendencies—the trends—of contemporary Christianity: well-intentioned tendencies that are puffed, acclaimed and approved here, there and everywhere, but which—let's face it—themselves need rigorous critical analysis.

II

God in the Rear: Up to Dateness Taken to Task

COME IN, EQUIVOCATOR!

A MAJOR and basic revision of Mother Church's entire armoury is under way. As usually happens, you spot a patch of rust on an old weapon and the superficial tarnish draws your eyes to other, less obvious signs of decay. By then the entire weapon seems to have had it; gradually the whole rack appears out of date; and—well, we might as well!—almost every item of equipment in the place is thrown out and the re-equipment plan is already devised, divided, sub-divided, and typed out in final copy.

A big display of tenacity, energy, bustle and movement; and apparently wherever there's so much movement, there must be life, initiative, and a real purpose in mind. That's quite a lot already for an institution that's hardly noted for smart work and quick decisions. Surely everyone can see that, all things considered, improvement, *aggiornamento*, being with it, refurbishing, whatever you call it, is worthwhile; that we already experience this renewal in a great number of good, really important, refreshing and even indispensable ways? After all, a thorough spring cleaning hardly ever succeeds unless the housewife or cleaner takes a certain furious pleasure in it. Yes, it's understandable—this sudden emotional uplift that has affected contemporary Christians: even when—as with some fast young priests— the feast threatens to degenerate into a first-class saturnalia in which everything that breaks the trammels of order seems to be allowed and even recommended, as long as it's modern and open-minded. Faced with this creative "destruction" and inspired "spring cleaning", you don't have to be particularly profound to ask what sort of gold reserves are there to back up all the paper money.

Whenever any conversion work was done on the structure of the Church in the past, it certainly entailed at least some connection with a deeper kind of conversion; and the deeper the incision made by conversion, the more extensive the pain. So it must be; unless it cuts deep there's probably more useless bloodletting than actual therapy. How much are we really prepared to pay for our reformation? Not only with the currency of things that don't count for much with us (historical prestige, for instance), but with items whose removal must cut us to the quick? Or were we just thinking of some kind of vague adaptation to circumstances? In fact, the outlook in all the undertakings at present in vogue is rather frenetic. We've got to jerk ourselves out of that splendid isolation at any price; we can see now that it was a dismal sort of half-existence. So let's forge ahead: dialogues and fraternizations, unseat the rulers from their thrones, drag the idols from their pedestals; let's collegialize, democratize, enlighten, level-down (there's no such thing as levelling-*up*), modernize at top speed. Zoom! Off we go, into a contemporary, ultra-contemporary, fabulous world of tomorrow and the day after tomorrow.

Surely no one would deny that the toppling process and the abandonment of heights held for so long had in most

26

cases been expected for a considerable time; it's all something that had to come: a long overdue process of recovery, and the very original change of heart recommended in the New Testament by which the "greatest among you" become the servants of all. Christ clearly prohibited all titles (such as "Sir", "Father", "Your Grace", "Abba", "Your Eminence", and so on); although he was our Lord, he humbled himself to become the servant of all men. As long as the present process is clearly the one that is long overdue—a genuine making up for lost time—then it's certainly a matter for self-congratulation. But we still have to ask after the motives for this hasty revision.

The Church, so it's said, must justify faith and respect by being in tune with the times. Basically, this must mean that Christ himself was in tune with the times when he carried out his mission by becoming a nuisance and a scandal to Jews and Gentiles, and dying on the cross. Of course the scandal occurred at the right time: at the moment chosen by the Father and in the fullness of time; just when Israel was ready, the fruit had come to maturity and the nations of the world were ready to receive it on their open soil.

But Jesus Christ was never up to date, and never will be. Neither he nor his disciples Paul and John said one word in favour of the latest political or gnostic doctrine. It's quite plain that the motive of all our renewals can only be a desire to get rid of the false, un-Christian scandals in the world in order to emphasize all the more clearly the true scandal that the Church is charged to show to the world. No one kind of therapy is justifiable.

Now we have something like a criterion for picking out those behind the contemporary trend in the Church. Christians would do well to realize that precisely because all these basic concerns seem straightforward and claim that the Christian crisis is an urgent necessity, they are two-edged and equivocal. They are possibly dangerous, too, since they pretend to be clear statements of all that is necessary, and reassuringly dispense men's consciences from the true conversion in depth.

The crisis doesn't come before or after a Christian initiative has been taken: it's one with it. And so it questions the nature of these very initiatives: are they directed towards God or away from him? Are they undertaken in a sincere attempt to reach God, or with God pushed right into the background?

To certain Christian reformers at the present moment keeping God in the rear means already knowing all there is to know about God, his revelation, its implications and extent, and about the Church and Christian people. It means sallying out, armed with this ready-made knowledge, to take part in encounters with the world: fellow Christians, non-Christians and anti-Christians. Such people believe the knowledge they carry with them is secure and adequate, even if it's really only summary—reduced to a few basic concepts. But the reduction is a legitimate one, to be sure: it's done with the planned dialogue with the contemporary world—or, as our theologians like to emphasize (with that disarming smile that serves to disclaim all suspicion of a tautology), with the contemporary secular world in mind. They know all there is to know about God and revelation; for them the question is a simple one: "How shall I put it to my children?" Leaving God behind them, they begin their advance towards the secular world: God's in his background and all's right since the world is before them. They wouldn't dispute that to be sent out into the world by Christ you have first of all to spend the right amount of time with him. They just think their training course has lasted long enough. Finding their proper vocation in action they tell themselves and others they're finished with contemplation. And should their knowledge tell them that they have passed no examination in contemplation or have even failed their finals, they're soon reassured by the old tag "*active* contemplation"; for the real proof of one's maturity is one's ability to act.

Many contemporary Christians—priests and laity—support themselves with this conviction. Unfortunately there has been too much self-conviction, for they go so far as to persuade themselves that their flight away from God is a mission from God. This is the extreme nature of the present Church crisis, in general and in particular. It's not so much a matter of condemning the crisis as plan, movement and results achieved, but of criticizing it from a Christian viewpoint. The external straightforwardness conceals a basic equivocation: being on one's way from God to the world *can* be an authentic Christian vocation; but it can also be flight from God, fear of the scandal of the cross, and renunciation of Jesus Christ. Everything has its other side: only Jesus is absolutely straightforward.

TREND TOWARDS THE BIBLE

The emphasis on the word of God is lauded as the most welcome and unequivocally hopeful sign in the Catholic world today. There's no denying the truth of this. Here it's quite clear that drawing back the drapes and hangings which obscure any attempt to see through to the origins of Christianity (the obfuscation brought about by all the later ecclesiastical, catechetical and dogmatic formulations of revelation) is a move *toward* the truth of God and Christ. In this way (now that he's finally allowed to), the Catholic tries to "hear, see and touch" the "Word of life". Rather bewildered, we stand in front of the darkness of the past: there were so many barbed-wire entanglements round the scriptures that anyone touching them was mortally scared of the electric shock of excommunication: like the people of Israel who dared not touch the foot of Sinai lest they die. Even the thousand-year-old wall of the Vulgate version, which prevented access to the original texts long, long after the work of the humanist scholars on them, has now fallen. Many approach the promised land of the original texts for the first time, and translations and commentaries multiply in answer to the general desire to understand. The Church certainly has its hands full if it is to satisfy this thirst for the word of God and help to make sure that it is pure and undefiled. A difficult job when, in conjunction with non-Catholic and non-Christian researchers, it has only just begun to examine the scriptures in accordance with the basic principles of modern historico-literary criticism.

The joy shown at this breakthrough ought not to be dampened but perhaps a little chastened at the thought that behind all the scholarship and ecclesiastical lore, the modern Catholic bible movement—like that of Martin Luther—does not owe its impetus primarily to a basic longing for God's original word; instead, the driving force has been largely the realization of judicious exegetes that Catholic biblical scholarship couldn't continue as it was without becoming the laughing-stock of the entire scholarly world. Oh, the delicacy with which the leaking tub of modern Catholic exegesis had to be steered between the

Scylla and Charybdis of threats of ecclesiastical condemnation—and this until very recently! But at last it reached the comparative safety of free and practical research. As scholarship began to breathe freely once more, the sense of release began to have widespread effects. These in turn had a beneficial influence on research itself. But we mustn't forget the chastening thought that Catholics have taken so long to leave this particular kind of isolation—well behind others outside our Church who were long ago co-operating in biblical studies at least.

Everything apart from Christ has its other side, and even the apparent straightforwardness of the renewal in biblical studies has its dark side. Once, in the immediate past, the Catholic viewpoint wasn't so uniform: between the wars there was a call for renewal when, behind the somewhat wooden discipline of a (new) scholasticism, the slogan was "back to the Fathers of the Church!" In many cases this "patristic spring" was no more than a spurious aestheticism. It just wasn't critical enough to last long. Now we have the patristic autumn (the "biblical spring") when there's a tendency to put the whole exegetical tradition, both patristic (first neo-Platonic then political or, rather, Constantinian and scholastic), under the suspicion now accorded the "purely theoretical"—a judgment not very different in fact from Luther's condemnation of the "whore of reason". Of course our latter-day moralists forget that thinking necessarily involves philosophizing; that anyone who omits a rigorous analysis of his premises is a ready victim to a crude ideology: that of "modern man", for instance.

The Catholic movement back to the origins meets with another contemporary movement, in the opposite direction: the swift-flowing Protestant surge from the Bible towards contemporaneity, which has marked out "modern man" as its horizon and criterion, and "modern philosophy" (Heidegger) as its instrument for interpreting sacred scripture. Whatever the "modern man" can grasp, whatever his senses allow him to take in, whatever helps and suits him religiously speaking—that's the gospel to preach; the rest is so much mythical rubbish to be discarded. The equivocation of this position is clear: the worst and the best are equally possible. The worst, inasmuch as the "modern man" (a mythical quantity if there ever was one!) is set up as the standard for what the word of God may and may not say, and what can be expected and not expected of a man. The best, in so far as the stimulus is there to re-experience and represent for each age, to take the whole revelation to heart and to make it personally relevant.

The Catholic return to the origins enters territory that is as little virgin land as Canaan when the people of Israel found it already inhabited. War didn't come at once, but after peace had been concluded co-existence with the Canaanites became more problematical, even ominous.

Seen from a total perspective this unexpected danger in the middle of a victorious crusade is thoroughly healthy and curative. It means that everyone is required to take the word of God for what it is: a call to make an absolute decision. Who is not for me is against me; and vice versa. If scientific neutrality is your slogan, then you can be active only in the frontline; and the man who dawdles too long before the battle line seems to be dodging the issue, or saying No to the request for a firm decision but trying to hide the fact behind his pseudo-scientific attitude.

God in the Rear: Up to Dateness Taken to Task

The liturgical renewal in the Church is one of the happiest of recent phenomena : it has countered the opposition of secularists and brought in a new emphasis on things that were always there. The results of liturgical renewal, of this apparently isolated ecclesiastical event, simultaneously affect the whole structure of the Church and its living acknowledgement of itself as the people of God and the body and bride of Christ. A central nerve has been touched and the reaction is felt in every limb of the entire organism.

Not the clergy but the community or congregation, the *ecclesia* made actual by gathering together, celebrates the memorial meal in which its Lord is bodily present and truly joins those present at the assembly who feed on his body to his body, making them one with him. The requirements for this kind of meeting of the community round the table of the Lord are satisfied in various ways. It proceeds in the order set out by St Paul (1 Cor. 11-14—although there's nothing said there about officially approved texts) and the way which Ignatius of Antioch would seem to have managed best : the community assembled about its presbyter. There is an extensive division of duties and roles that is part of the ecclesiastical charisma. The Bible is read to the people in a language they understand, and explained to them in a homily; the homily is therefore a faithful interpretation and not an address or "sermon" on any desired theme. The space in which the church meets, as soon as it has to be larger than an ordinary room, answers the needs of this kind of assembly of the community round the Lord's table, with regard to its ground-plan, seating, altar, chancel, font, the practical and decorative apparatus, and

B 33

so on. It must be clear that all that has been achieved to-day is the result of reconsideration of essential and self-evident aspects of the Christian community.

But it's not all straightforward: some older people can't find their way through the new services and are inclined to resist changes, not only out of a feeling for tradition, but because they find that certain values are now absent; indeed, they find those they prized most highly have been earmarked for exclusion. What do they regret? The spiritual freedom of the silence within which the mystery was enclosed. Aren't we all present (so they say) at the enactment of the most incomprehensible of all things incomprehensible? Isn't it true that beyond space and historical time, the very centre of all time is present, as God's own Son, burdened with the sins of the world, with my own sins, passes under God's judgment into everlasting night? There's no "community" in this event; only a collection of sinful individuals, of whom I am one. How can this particular later community, which takes its light from the tremendous force of that apocalyptic and paradoxical eclipse, think of celebrating its own moment of birth as something happening now, let alone celebrate it in faith and sacramentally, without abasing itself in an attitude of total adoration?

Where are the worship and adoration in our up to date services? Thinking either that these functions are superfluous or that churchgoers aren't mature enough, the clergy have taken it into their heads to fill out the time in a practical way and with a pretty varied run of activities: there's not a moment left free. Noisy all the time; if it's not prayers out loud or Bible readings and expositions, then it's singing and responses that have to be listened to; even the Canon of the Mass booms out of the loudspeaker—in

English, too! They seem to have forgotten that almost no one present has any time or opportunity during the week to collect himself together in really deep devotion; that souls must recreate themselves individually at Sunday Mass, and find a spiritual breathing-space; that God speaks loudest in a still, small voice—in silence; that the service of God's Word admittedly includes the word of God—as gospel and prayer—but that the act of lifting up the mind and heart and of personal affirmation in silence is indispensable lest everything should fall on stony ground and among the thorns.

Undoubtedly a satisfactory communal service also brings about a kind of fulfilment. The priest is pleased with the congregation for co-operating efficiently; the congregation is pleased with itself for receiving the benefits of a spiritual feast. Yes, that's the Church, pleased with itself: the spiritual self-satisfaction of the congregation. But that's what we've always held against the Protestants: a pietistic, liberal prayer-service that makes you all feel self-satisfied as you pour out smiling at one another! Is Karl Barth right after all with his malicious conjunction of Schleiermacher and Catholicism—the Mystical Body in self-glorifying celebration? Or what about those sinister comments in papers and periodicals? This one, for instance: "I believe that God has become all too human in the hearts of all too many people and that there is a new kind of secularization afoot which centres this time not upon material secularization but morality. In this way humanity becomes the subject and object of its own glorification, but in the guise of the Christian religion of love. . . . This intellectual morality is allied to the international development of human consciousness and appears . . . in two forms: firstly, with the Enlightenment, as a secular, progressively oriented ethic of solidarity; and, secondly, in the above-mentioned contemporary Christian self-celebration of humanity in the name of God."[5]

TREND TOWARDS ECUMENISM

The separation of the Churches is the greatest public scandal in Christendom. There is no excuse for its cause or for its result: the unworthy witness of Christian home and foreign missions. Everything that helps to repair the breaches is in accordance with the will of God. That long maintained positions should have been abandoned and that an apparently hopeless lack of communication should have been overcome in so singular a way can be interpreted only as a miraculous working of the grace of God's Spirit, who has heard the prayers and answered the anguish of Christians on both sides.

We must do all we can while acknowledging the process as the working of the all-powerful Creator Spirit. Since we have begun to hope so effectively, let us take courage from our hope and continue despite all setbacks and the notorious "impossibilities". Only the spirit of Jesus can throw down the wall that divides us; we ourselves cannot do it: not with all the goodwill in the world, not with all our slick theological diplomacy. It seems appropriate at this point to consider the hidden equivocation in our own procedure, and to see the crisis of the word of God as the world sees it first. Is it so difficult to do all we can ourselves to bring about unity in Christ and at the same time to do nothing in a merely human way to coerce the Spirit "technically"?

Perhaps it seems obvious that we should concentrate on the points we're agreed on and let all that separates us fade into the background. That would be more acceptable to

Reformed opinion, for which the matters that separate consist more of a minus than a plus, whereas we Catholics are credited with unjustifiable additions to the simple message of the gospels.

The difficulty for Protestants is to see how this Catholic plus can frankly be added to the Gospel. Therefore it would seem to be the duty of Catholics to awaken the understanding of a possible clear connection, and then undertake an examination of the evidence. But how? It can justly be said that all ecclesiastical phenomena, even the statements of dogma, are relative to the absolute point of the revelation of God in Christ. The body is relative to its head, the Eucharist to the Last Supper and the cross, the mother to the Son, purgatory to the judgment of Christ; the authority of the Church is properly relative only to the priesthood of Christ; and those who hold office in the Church must realize that we have one Master, but we are all brothers. Every dogma is relative to the truth of revelation which it seeks to present—periphrastically, summarily, validly—but not exhaustively. This relativity is best shown to our separated brothers by living it : just as John XXIII lived the relativity of the highest office in the Church and impressed it on the whole world. Or as each Council has shown the true relativity of a dogma, not by compromise but by putting it in a new context : giving it a new angle of vision, so that its absolute nature is softened by seeing it in the context of the fluctuation of human thought, or discussion about the word of God. In this way, but no less effectively, the Marian teachings have been set in the total framework of the teaching on the Church as a whole.

But this last example clearly shows the alternative. What does "making relative" mean in this case? In what spirit, with what intention and what motivation is it undertaken? Is the purpose to adjust the dimmer for the Marian dogmas, to obscure them, even to juggle them out of sight, while other more significant lights are suddenly switched full on, rather like the fading and disappearance of the stars at sunrise? Does this mean that there really has been a change? Not only that practical infelicities and excesses of uninformed devotion have occurred (which no reasonable man denies) but that *theoretically* the essential truth has been extended much too far? This would be the above-mentioned method of subtraction or levelling down. Where this process is already followed, it offends sensibilities on both sides: on this side, because Catholics themselves aren't clear how the Church can let go of things that it has maintained vehemently for centuries, even for thousands of years. On the other side, because it smells of canting diplomacy—the sort of thing one might justifiably expect from the Vatican with its long history of political manoeuvring. Perhaps the dialogue is merely exoteric or superficial, and therefore a trap which will snap to as soon as anyone has ventured inside the masked jaws.

No, the second way is not the path of ecumenism. The first way must be taken, and taken to the end. But it's much more demanding and spiritually exacting. It requires Catholics to make a doubly intensive theological effort. First of all the straightforward delineation on both sides of all those aspects of theology, proclamation and devotional practice which other Christians will accept as genuine (even if different) expressions of the Christian revelation which both sides acknowledge. The doctrine of justification by faith alone once seemed an extremely divisive point, but the necessary reassessment has already been taken a long way; it must be taken all the way. Then —on the other side as well—we need a basic reassessment of individual positions: so thorough that the very rigour of the analysis carried out on our own beliefs will possibly allow comprehension of the other side's viewpoint. But all this can advance only on the basis of a spiritual effort and strain which should certainly not be imposed equally on every member of the Church; above all, it cannot be forced on the laity. Nevertheless the various stages of thought and discussion and their results must be generally accepted so that everyone is party to the process of reunion without being able to complain about strategic compromises and diplomatic ruses.

But the most important requirement for such a venture is that both partners in the dialogue have God before them and not behind them. All movement must be towards God, the depth of whose wisdom and mystery appears always to increase. Today, I think, Catholics are beginning once again to discover that as one tries to look into it the mystery of God becomes all the greater in depth. In the actual process of ecumenical dialogue, perhaps they will learn that God's revelation can't be neatly bottled and laid down in the cellar; that the vintage answers brought up from the vaults of the past just don't suit the very exacting and practical palates of the present; that, despite ecclesiastical tradition and the infallible teaching office of the Church, world history moves forward inexorably; that providential moments can occur only on the basis of a full personal decision; and that—a difficult task indeed—the entire tradition of the Church must ever and again be melted down into the historical moment, and reconceived and shaped in accordance with the nature of that moment. Then we are assured of the help of the Holy Spirit; we begin to see the marks of his action, and to understand what tradition really is: something that can never take

39

shape without martyrdom, without the risk of life and death in a total act of witness.

But in such dialogues, the definition of a Christian appears as something in the future rather than something to be forced from the concepts of the past. The Catholic does not enter into dialogue by making minor concessions, subtracting this part from his "plus quantity", abandoning that part; instead he must carry out his unremitting analysis in the light of the basic gospel of Jesus Christ.

TREND TOWARDS THE "SECULAR" WORLD

Here is the high and mid point of the movement. Here the decisive and saving breakthrough must occur : in the abrogation and transformation of a sterile tendency towards self-preservation in the Church. In the process of breaking out and breaking into the world (so the argument runs) it must reach an understanding of its essential nature; must therefore make clear what a Christian really is.

This viewpoint is supported and underlined by historical comparisons. Once, in earlier times—it is alleged—there was no secular world but only a cosmos that men conceived of wholly in a religious fashion : as some say, they "divinized" it. Under the protection of a primitive religious illusion men thought of the deity as being close to them and present throughout nature. This fond dream has been rudely shattered in the world of modern technology where nature is under man's control. The world has been "demythologized" and totally "humanized"; and this is the cold, disenchanted world which the Christian is required to enter without fear and without reservation.

This entrance into the world is made to seem all the more difficult when the definite and undeniable flight from reality by Catholics after the French Revolution and in the early nineteenth century is enlarged to serve as an image for the general Christian attitude throughout the past. This is certainly unjust, since a Christian openness to the world was apparent not only in the apostolic endeavours of the first Christians, but also in the questionable and nowadays harshly criticized century in which the Roman empire and its imperialistic apparatus were christianized, in the conversion of barbarians, in the reclamation of their forests and deserts by monks and orders of knights, in the attachment to this world of great Western art, philosophy and literature, and in the permeation by a new ethic of the organization of cultures and empires. Surely in all this, reformers and purists have found too much rather than too little attachment and adaptation to the world.

But we are referred too to the ascetic movements of the past : and certainly in their earlier phases these were distinguished by a movement away from the world, beginning with an impressive retreat of the spiritual aristocracy into the wilderness, hermitages and conventual cells, continuing with the treatises of the medieval cloisters on religious contempt of this world, and arriving eventually at the more modern evidence of the life of renunciation shown in the evangelical counsels. But all this (it's now pointed out emphatically), by a subtle Christian instinct, has brought about an increasing tendency to turn towards the world.

The first monks' flight from the world into pure contemplation resulted in the Benedictines and their emphasis on cultivation; they were followed by the preaching and evangelistic orders which, with the Society of Jesus, abandoned the life of the cloisters and engaged themselves very practically in the affairs of this world. Today the secular

institutes lead the way by following the evangelical counsels while living their worldly vocation; in no way are they
separated from the world. If it's true that for so long a
time the vanguard of Christianity followed precisely this
route, then this impressive swing from the cell far from
civilization to a life of full engagement with the secular
community is an unmistakably decisive judgment of the
Holy Spirit. Anyone who is fully aware of the dynamic
movement of the modern world will not fail to draw the
moral from this unceasing forward movement: it was
thought for a long time that the "evangelical counsels"
had to be taken literally; but they are intended mainly in
a spiritual sense, and are realized fully—without the extreme of external virginity—in the full humanity of unfailing co-operation in Christian marriage. Similarly, the
external poverty of former times finds full human shape
in a true sense of "indifference" to all possessions; and the
true fulfilment of eternal childhood is found in the
humility of the fully responsible Christian layman living
a full life in this world, yet courageously following the
dictates of his conscience.

To begin to fit together the background to the present
trend, one has only to support these assertions by suggest-
ing the presence of a latent "manichaean" attitude of opposition to sex in early and medieval Christians—the traces
of which are unfortunately only too clear in ecclesiastical
injunctions and repressive legislation with regard to marriage; has only to point out the understandable obedience
of a still childlike and hardly educable mankind to a patern-
ally oppressive ecclesiastical authority—an attitude which
has been superseded in the natural process of maturity;
finally, need only add that in an age of increasing special-
ization, competence in individual fields is more and more

the affair of trained professionals. For practical reasons, such specialists have increasingly to abandon past forms of submission to ecclesiastical authorities: as an obvious consequence, the latter must restrict themselves to purely spiritual matters.

The dominant emphasis in the Church is therefore shifting irresistibly from the clergy and clerical authorities to the layman; and the layman, in so far as he is the Church open to and enclosed within the activity of the world, is the real centre of God's kingdom on earth. The priest, on the other hand, is only an assistant—a technical assistant whose advisory role is limited to existing as a symbolic reminder to laymen that they and the world are not the whole picture, that the kingdom of God has not finally come, but that the "future" of the Lord will be fully and openly realized only in the final transformation at the end of time. The life of renunciation, too, is only symbolic: the emphasis is on the life of engagement as the way proper to being a human. Similarly, the official shepherd of the Church is there only for the sake of his flock: his whole ability and power are to be used for the sake of his flock and to help them thrive.

If, in establishing this attitude to the world, we take into account the theory of biological evolution and its simple (naïve!) transference to the field of natural and supernatural human history, the tendency becomes irresistible. Does this mean that it is the task of man himself to undertake the development of the cosmos, by active spiritual planning to guide history towards its completion and, in this way, as far as possible to prepare and "accelerate" the future of the Lord?

With this shift in emphasis we happen on an unexpected and apparently incidental answer to our main question,

"Who is a Christian?". In the context of the above-mentioned discussion, the answer is: the man who most deeply engrains what is Christian into the stuff of the modern world, who most basically "incarnates" it in the world. Is there any need then for the channels of grace we have relied on for so long: the Bible, the sacraments, preaching the word, and so on? Surely they must be converted into life and action, a process that occurs in everyday Christian life—i.e., the common secular life. This then is the fulfilment of the parable of the leaven and those gnomic sayings about the salt of the earth and the light of the world.

It all seems so simple and obvious: so liberating, too (from the pressure of clericalism and the regimentation of an anti-worldly asceticism). In a very encouraging sense it seems to demand from us as much effort as possible. Indeed, the equivocation of this particular tendency almost disappears beneath so much that is positive and enlivening.

But the essential ambiguity reappears if we ask these new "secular Christians" what exactly is the content of the Christianity they hope to incarnate in the world. If you've defined a concept once you can't incorporate your old explanation in a new definition. And you already have (behind you) a concept of what Christianity is (and therefore of what a Christian is), with which you operate when planning your action in relation to the world. For you're surely not going to claim that being open to the world is in itself the content of Christianity? You yourselves are fragments of the world, and so you don't need to open yourselves to it. Something like this peculiar feat of acrobatics might at most be ascribed to God, who of himself is not the "world" and in his turning to the world confers grace upon the world. For you, on the other hand, existence in the world is your nature and a spiritual duty

44

inherent in your condition. Perhaps the contented, responsible and devoted way in which you intend to co-operate in the world process is the Christian spirit you want to contribute to it? But this spirit, however admirable, certainly doesn't in any essential way surpass what ought to be required of every member of the human community.

Perhaps you would claim that the particular degree of your concern for the common welfare of all and of your devotion to your fellow men is what is really Christian; that men will recognize it in an especially pure, clear and arresting expression of humanity? You could bring forward some pretty impressive support for such a viewpoint: that Christianity doesn't consist of external practices and churchgoing, but is the fulfilment of the real desire of Jesus which he made clear for us when, for example, he washed his disciples' feet. We should all be brothers, serving and helping one another, just as Jesus did when he was our Lord. This means that we should differentiate ourselves from other men not by any features peculiar to ourselves, but only by answering the demands of a universal common humanity and solidarity more conscientiously and consistently than others. And if the task of humanity in this "finally" quite secular world is precisely the spiritual and technical development of this world by mankind, then it's up to Christians to lead the way by good example and keep at the forefront of the common effort. Instead of always arriving too late on the scene, having spent the time with our eyes raised to heaven while down below and all round us the great opportunities of world history are being missed one after the other, we can at last come alive to the religious needs of the present age and set an example in so doing.

Would Communism have ever been necessary if Chris-

tians had realized their responsibilities at the right time?
Wouldn't human concern for the poor and exploited have
been in accordance with the spirit of the Old and New
Testaments? And if there hadn't been those fatal connections between the capitalist exploiters and the Christian religion, would modern atheism ever have been
necessary?

Here we meet with the fact ". . . that the proletarian
movement had almost of necessity to be atheistical, because God was not evident during the decisive years of its
origin. Apart from and after Christ himself, God was
evident only in Christians who followed Christ. But
Christianity, which no longer offered the support of a
protective social order for the peasantry and the ordinary
citizen, was now evident in no protective role whatsoever.
It was only too prominent however in justification of and
as a weapon of the exploiters themselves. That there was
no God . . . was not a logical conclusion, but the clear
evidence of experience. The anti-religious, revolutionary
atheism that marked the origins of the working-class
movement was directly influenced by the absence of God,
that is by the absence of Christians."[6]

What ought to have been done? What was needed? A
firm sense of human brotherhood, instead of a pharisaical
"practice of Christianity" in a way blind to the realities
of the human condition. What was the point of all the
supernatural flummery—that out of touch concern for
the hereafter—when a Christian's duty was obviously
there, right in front of his nose, waiting to be done? And
isn't this just as true today as it was at the time of the
Communist Manifesto? How many of the demands of
basic humanity remain unanswered because people obviously have no time for them: here is the opening for the

Christian; here is his chance to make his religion incarnate.

Despite the truth of this, the essential question must be raised again: is Christianity no more than the consistent practice of humanism? If it is, we have to admit that the serious, decent theology of the Enlightenment and liberalism was right after all: Christ is the most accomplished teacher of humanity—its pre-eminent example and model. Since Christ showed us the way, we *know* what genuine solidarity and selflessness are. Since we know that, what is the point of faith? Isn't it enough to try to realize the plain directives of the Sermon on the Mount? They are not mysterious in themselves, but make demands on our whole existence. What on earth is the point of adding dogmatic mysteries of faith? Love of our fellow men can become our inner spiritual life. Why should we bother with these "pronouncements" which we're asked to take as literal truth and which remain completely detached from our human experience? All right, being a Christian means achieving something: but if we are able to achieve only what we understand and can make an active response to, why must we add something that's incomprehensible—a crude diet of indigestible and unnecessary roughage?

Here the question "Who is a Christian?" is posited most clearly. If my existence as a Christian has to be service to and in the secular world, I must be able to obtain and understand a clear guide to what I'm expected to do. It must be in accordance with human reason and the human power of action. Having received my orders of the day, I go into action. I've read and understood my guidelines before leaving them behind me, even though I'm continually faced with the necessity of acting on them in the context of each new situation. This is the *a priori* aspect of the fourth tendency. It is indeed a tendency towards

47

action, but it relies on a hidden abstraction: the Christian content is (nothing more than) the truly human.

This *a priori* content can be concealed in various ways. One is to take the world which has only just been demythologized, and to see it again in a theological guise by talking about, say, a "theology of secular reality". Such a way of looking at the world is possible only when one has first of all (in something like the sense intended by St Thomas Aquinas) defined it "philosophically". But nowadays the stress in philosophy is on a more "exact science" of naked facts. Without the mediation of real philosophical method, this science is abruptly confronted with theology. This kind of procedure can never produce more than the *appearance* of debate—and in fact this simulated discussion always turns out to be the application of a vapid and half-hearted dialectic. "Creation as Salvation" and "Creation as the Mystery of Salvation" are fair samples of the favourite themes and titles of certain modern books. They sound promising, but they rely on a short-circuit, an equation of philosophy with theology; and in this kind of confusion theology always gets the worst of it.

The most contradictory positions are reconciled in these easy syntheses; but only superficially and without any genuine mediation. Nowadays, in the same breath of conviction, we hear it announced that the world has been finally demythologized and has become purely secular; and yet that it must be perceived as a total eucharistic mystery, as the evolving mystical body of Christ: a mythologization and "divinization" of the cosmos far beyond anything that the medieval realists provided for in their Christian philosophy of the universe. But (in these naïve syntheses) the creation is—in its evolutionary aspect as well—conceived of directly as a theological and sacramental mystery; and, in spite of their previous demythologization, all secular and worldly processes are immediately transformed into spiritual processes. To all intents and purposes, this implies no more than that the processes of the world are subject only to man's technical mind and his way of perceiving them : the world that has been demythologized to the point of atheism is, as such, also the world made sacred to the point of divinizing it. But these are just empty phrases : a noisy chatter with which Christians deceive themselves in the contemporary world —a world which can get along very well without them while, in all innocence, they're doing no more than chuck sand in their own eyes. If you've already secretly cancelled the distinctions, it's absolutely pointless to pretend you can still maintain them; it's ludicrous to think you're saying something deeply meaningful in any Christian sense, when you call the secular "spiritual", and the spiritual "secular".

It's useful to take a look at Christian tradition, whose impressive witness I mentioned at the beginning of this section, and decide whether to tax it with excessive secularism ("mythologization" of the world), or excessive withdrawal from the world ("demythologization" of the world). If the charge doesn't hold, then it should be clear that Christianity in the past, through concepts and forms of expression suited to particular cultures, has seen and represented both aspects of reality. No one can deny that the fate of the cosmos as a whole was always part of the understanding and feeling of the Christian interpretation of existence. It is impossible to reproach the strongest and most effective cosmogonies with "antipathy to the cosmos", or repudiation of the world. The "holy cosmos", i.e. the world, which through God's creation, becoming

49

man, reconciliation and redemption, but also through the fulfilment of the worldly and human laws of existence, matures into the ultimate fullness of Jesus Christ, was the concern of Origen, Dionysius the Areopagite, Boethius and John Scotus Erigena, Fulbert of Chartres and the great scholastic theologians Albert, Bonaventure and St Thomas Aquinas. It was the concern of Nicholas of Cusa, of the thought of the Christian renaissance from Florence to Oxford, and of the baroque mysticism of Jakob Böhme and his school, right up to Schelling and Baader. Against all of these, with the possible exception of Augustine, one could more justifiably lay the objection that they put too much of the world in their spirituality, and too much philosophy in their theology. Precisely this makes one suspect complaints about escapism or even manichaeism in the ascetic tendencies of monasticism or the medieval counsel of poverty, and reject claims that the last traces of these undesirable features have been successfully expunged only in our glorious modern era. It is possible that these tendencies represent something like an antidote to an excessively secular Christianity, too entangled in politics as well as in philosophy, but—as an antidote— they are healthy and justifiable.

But surely we should have found out what a Christian really is before examining these four contemporary tendencies, since all four paths have proved equivocal and therefore rather dangerous roads to take? Surely we should first of all know what the question implies. We must turn about and place what is obviously behind us, before us. The right situation is to have the question paper as well as the answer script in front of us; for the answer must come from the very place from which the life of Christ shines forth: from the living word of God.

III

God Before Us, or: Who is a Christian?

THERE'S a useful and simple rule of logic: the real nature of something is best seized in its most obvious manifestation.[7] Anyone who seeks the nature of the horse or the ass in a mule will find himself in difficulties; anyone who tries to find out what a Christian is by studying a man who can't really decide whether to be one, who knows the demands made by Christianity but hasn't the courage to put them into practice, who knows quite well or feels that his behaviour isn't up to the standard required of a Christian, is working on inadequate evidence. This is much more obvious with this particular specimen—the Christian—than with anything else: for the basic decision required by the word of Christ is always before him. Christ asks men to make this decision, and it's not to be thought of merely as the entry door to the Christian life, which is then something to be found after the decision: it is already and initially one with the Christian life.

An examination of the various types of possible Christian attitude, from the lowest form of compromise (which can still share to a certain extent in the life of Christ) to the highest and most resolute form, undeniably shows that the Christian ideal shines out more clearly when a life is lived more decidedly in accordance with the precepts of Jesus. A straightforward saint (there are "warped" ones too) is no equivocator. He's the sort of man who from time to time gets the comment, "If only everyone was like you. . . ." It's precisely the "saint"—the man who tries to do everything as a Christian should do it—who knows best and most deeply how great a sinner he is. Others are very concerned about or resign themselves to the distance that separates them from full Christianity. And others are scrupulous; but the saint tries to see himself in the clear light of the grace and the commandment of love that come from God. He is ultimately humbled and bereft of all illusions about himself.

Who is a Christian? To get an answer it's no use playing with externals ("someone who's baptized", "someone who fulfils his Easter duties"). You have to go straight to the point—the focal point. The minimalist is a highly complex because unmethodical and opaque figure from whom you can't expect a clear answer. On the other hand, the maximalist—if only the term were used, but it isn't—offers the simple, translucent image; so simple that *he* is the true minimalist, because in him all the perplexities are integrated. According to St Paul the minimalist conceives of the moral law so much as a countless multitude of fixed commandments that he can't see the wood for the trees. For the maximalist, the man who directs his life towards Christ, all these negative commandments are reduced to one simple law; whoever follows it obeys all the others; and it's not, as Christ tells us, a difficult commandment to follow.

This methodical viewpoint deserves attention before any more problematical areas are opened up.

God Before Us, or: Who is a Christian?

The Christian takes his name from Christ. His nature stands and falls with the nature of Christ. But here we have to ask a difficult question: what kind of essential relationship—what kind of communion—can exist between Christ and Christians?

A primary and inescapable assertion for everyone who truly believes in Christ's life and work is that Christ is the only Son of the Father, the sole intermediary between God and men, and the only Saviour who on the cross has given satisfaction for all; the first-born (first-fruit) of those raised from the dead, who, according to St Paul, is the first principle of all things (Col. i. 19). What he is, what he does, what happens through him, is reconciled in the full nature of God. He actively redeemed us; we were passively reconciled by him. Everything that we do after that, actively, in recognition of what he did, must always rely on this initial passivity, recognizing it in faith and proclaiming it in witness. Bearing witness gives unity to our whole Christian existence and action. This assertion is so obvious that it's a cardinal principle of orthodox Reformed Christianity, and everything that can be added to it seems only to obscure it.

It is helpful to look at the account given in the New Testament. Looked at superficially, it could be seen as the record of a man who forces himself on public attention: someone with a talent for prophecy who proclaims the kingdom of God as he preaches, works miracles to win respect for his divine mission and then faith in him personally, and also chooses a small band of men to witness and record his words and actions; so that finally, when he has died and is risen from the dead, they can be witnesses

Who is a Christian?

to him ". . . in all Judea and Samaria, and to the very ends of the earth!" (Acts 1. 8). This initial aspect of Christianity is undeniable; it continues, for the command to witness closes the gospels of Matthew and Luke and opens the Acts of the Apostles, which, together with the Epistles, contain the record of this bearing witness to Christ.

But it doesn't stop there. Christ not only speaks and acts *in front of* men, but goes *with* them and invites them to go *with* him. This happens in a particularly obvious way with the choosing of the disciples: he "called to him those whom he desired; and they came to him. And he appointed twelve, to be with him . . ." (Mark 3. 13-14).

On other occasions when Christ summons men we find the words *sequere me*, which can be translated as "follow me" as long as the following is understood not in the sense of a trailing behind but a master-disciple relationship in which, by following him, the disciple is brought into the inner world of the master and initiated spiritually into a new life. The more you think about it, this being-with, this companionship, seems to be the predominant form of Christ's life on earth. He begins his human existence in the womb of his mother, who declared her acceptance of God's word; he spends his childhood in a family which he leaves for a few days in order to listen to and ask questions of the teachers. He begins his public life by collecting together a band of disciples; in front of three disciples he is transfigured in the company of Moses and Elijah, and is sorrowful and troubled before the same three on the Mount of Olives. He goes to the cross in the company of two other convicts who hang on either side of him. Even when he rises from the dead he's not alone, for the graves open on Good Friday, and on Easter Sunday "many bodies of the saints who had fallen asleep were raised, and coming out of their tombs after his resurrection they went into the holy city and appeared to many" (Matt. 27. 52-53). And when he has risen from the grave and walks with his disciples on the road to Emmaus, he proclaims to the last his message of companionship.

But being *with* becomes being *within*. The stage of companionship extends without cancellation to a third stage of final intimacy: to the inwardness that he works in the mystery of bread and wine, which he "earnestly desires" and has previously indicated in a number of signs and promises, and which is to be seen in unity with his saving death. This he anticipates absolutely and intentionally; he distributes himself as he dies to those who are with him, and enters into them as an undying life that is contemporary with all epochs of human history. His final prayer to the Father unmistakably emphasizes the state of inwardness that has been reached: they are all in him and he is in them, just as he is one with the Father. And he sets all his hope on this being one through being within: by it the world should recognize that he has been sent from God. In their mission of witness, the apostles take strength from their faithful awareness that they are in the Lord and that he is in them ("Christ lives in me").

These concepts have become so familiar that their paradoxical aspect has been overlooked: to the extent that the disciples bear witness to his unique existence *before* them, he remains in companionship *with* them and *within* them, to the very last. Not only that: the more he was *with* them, the more they grasped his uniqueness; the more he is *in* them and they live by and share in his life, the less they are confounded with him, and the higher he rises *above* them as the *kyrios*, the Lord.

The sense of distance increases with the degree of nearness. With insight into his incomprehensible humiliation, the understanding grows that inconceivable height and majesty are contained and shown forth in that very degradation. The more he shows his power in submission to suffering, the more clearly he proves that he alone has the power to lay down his life for the sake of the sheep and to take it up again (John 10. 16-18); therefore that he alone can suffer, die and rise from the dead on behalf of all other men. The disciple who on the basis of true companionship and intimacy with Jesus understands this in faith is continually referred forward to the necessity of bearing witness; simultaneously he is referred back to the unique power of the Lord to whom he bears this very witness.

Contemporary Christianity, tired of a merely external practice of religion, has concentrated its love and attention on the Christian who bears witness. *Témoignage* is the modish and almost excessively invoked catchword in France. The life of the worker priests was witness; the life of the Little Brothers and Sisters is witness; that of the new world organizations or "secular institutes" is witness; and so finally is every committed form of Christian existence in Church and world. However serious this kind of progress seems in comparison to the pharisaical religion of an effete bourgeoisie, and however fully the concept of "witness" comprehends the stages of companionship and inwardness (in the full concept of martyrdom), it can itself be taken in a minimalistic fashion, as the reflection of an historically conditioned phenomenon. In this sense—to take an extreme case—even a non-Christian could "bear witness" to the crucifixion and the "empty grave". And the eucharistic celebration of the Christian community could similarly be thought of as a thankful commemoration of the good effects of redemption; just as the victorious feat of Judith was celebrated annually by the Israelites and "received by the Hebrews in the number of holy days, and is religiously observed by the Jews from that time until this day" (Jud. 16. 31, Vulg.).

Of course, such an interpretation of the communal Eucharist is clearly inadequate; not only because Christians have (in the Holy Spirit) to live the word of God as something contemporary and progressive, but because in transformation and communion the "remembered" Lord is present in his physical and spiritual reality: before them, with them, in them.

This is the teaching of the Gospel and what the Christian believes. But the Christian also tries to understand what he believes: how is it possible that the unique and incomparable which is Christ should be not only before us, but with and in us? How do we genuinely co-operate with him, without the activity in which we take part ceasing to be the being and activity of the unique Lord? Here we are concerned not with mere pedantic subtleties but with the focal point: one that must be brought out if we are to obtain an answer to our original question. Here and nowhere else we shall find the content that will prove decisive in the ecumenical dialogue with Protestantism.

THE FOCAL POINT

Let's go back to the formal course of Jesus' life. His youth was the long preparation and gradual initiation of the mature man for his mission to the world; his baptism was his investiture with the Spirit and his actual mission; his spell in the wilderness and his temptation were his final existential test and confirmation. Now the candidate had completed his training and could begin his active ministry, and called some men to be his followers. They were to follow him not as spectators but as companions who would take part in the tremendous and absolute aspect of his existence. They were to expose themselves in his act of self-exposure: he made this clear when he told them at the Last Supper: "You are those who have continued with me in my *trials* . . ." (Luke 22. 28). They did it of their own free will, for they had the opportunity to leave him alone to his fate.

This community of full faith in discipleship might seem almost no more than the human virtue in a relationship between, say, a feudal lord and his retainer. But since Jesus is, does and asks more than a human being, the loyalty shown by his disciples is also more than human attachment: it is faith. But both forms of loyalty would not have been united if Jesus had not carried out his supreme action in a human form—and therefore a form basically open and accessible to human beings: the form of absolute obedience to God.

Jesus doesn't follow his own but the Father's will. He declares this by tears and bloody sweat on the Mount of Olives, while he encloses his human will—beyond the limits of his desire and ability—in the will of the Father. This obedience goes beyond the bounds of all human power by extending into God's everlastingness; it is the free choice of the form of a servant, and the choice is made and the form taken by the eternal, threefold love between Father and Son in the Holy Spirit. This is a supreme decision of love not to hold fast (as St Paul says) to its own divine form but to let it pass into the narrow confines of human form, the anonymity of a plain individual life, and finally an obedience to God unto death—even to an ignominious death on a cross. Obedience on a basis of love given right up to the most extreme consequences is the form taken by the life of God made man. And this "median" state offers ordinary men a way of sharing in the life, activity and suffering of God made man.

This free obedience in love is the point where the incompatibles meet and achieve a common identity. For men this loving obedience is faith. And faith, as a human act, is an inchoate attempt at self-surrender ("Lord, I believe, help thou mine unbelief"); but when the Lord encloses it in his own obedience and mercifully receives it into the power of his own example and standard, then at the first attempt it is successful and finds fulfilment (*gratia praeveniens* and *consequens*). If we look for an analogous situation in the purely human sphere, I suppose we might think of a girl awakened by a young man's unmistakable love, her definite consent to this power of love in the young man and the way in which her consent is sustained until fulfilment. But perhaps there are unconscious bounds to this display of human surrender (however unlimited she thinks it is); for if the man to whom she made her submission now shows a complete lack of faith, denies the love he gave her and chooses evil, a covenant with him is no longer tolerable. Faith in Christ, on the other hand, is a form of surrender without bounds; the boundlessness is the test of the faith.

Since any lack of faith is impossible on Christ's side, even when his loyalty became invisible for us in the dark night of the crucifixion when he was completely forsaken; since of its very nature God's loyalty is unending and without regret: the act of faith—loving, obedient submission to the power of God's grace which allows it and makes it possible—can be unconditional and unlimited. In its fullness, this act is called faith, hope and love : loving faith, which hopes for everything that God wills; faithful hope, which loves everything that God wills; hoping love, which believes everything that God wills. This act is the basis and essence of the Christian life, and so—unexpectedly— we have found the answer to our question "Who is a Christian?" A Christian is the man who "lives by faith" (Rom. 1. 17), which means that he has staked his whole existence on the one opportunity that Jesus Christ, the Son of God, obedient for us all unto the cross, has given him : to share in his own universally saving, obedient sub- mission to God.

On Christ's side the act of obedience comes from love, for the Son of God does not take on human existence as the result, so to say, of a sudden movement started by an external motor : he becomes an empirical being by virtue of his mission of love. Christ takes on human reality *as* the manifestation of God the Father's love for us; the Father who *is*, yet sends his Son to *exist* for us sinners. The devotion is in this taking on of our ordinary human life; and in the devotion is the acceptance of sacrifice— the obedience.

And so in the existence of the obedient Son the mystery of the divine Trinity shines forth in its full brightness. The Son is obedient not to himself, but to another—but out of an eternal love; and this eternal love makes possible such obedience and, at the same time, the unity of the Father who orders and the Son who obeys. If the Son were obedient on the basis of a natural inferiority to God the Father, then in being obedient he would only be doing his duty, and not manifesting the absolutely free love of God. But if he obeys "without reason"—in other words, out of pure love—then in the Christ who is sent to us there appears the groundless love for us sinners of the Father who sends him : a love so groundless that St Paul does not hesitate to call it foolish. And if after giving evidence of his love by inscribing the sign of his love in human history; if after the life, death and resurrection of the sacrificed Son, the Spirit common to Father and Son is sent out from them into the Church and into the world as an everlasting witness of the event, then this Spirit will never be and never bear witness to any love other than that which is groundless and foolish, and therefore never open or subject to all the clever machinations of men.

The essence of this love appears in the human existence of the Son as the renunciation of his self-will. Only this renunciation of self gives his mission and the way he carries it out its scandalously explosive quality. He gave up all discretion or "fore-sight" and resigned providence to the Father who sent and guided him. He abandoned all thought of calculation, management and diplomacy. And it's precisely this self-renunciation, surrender and emptying that provides the never failing impetus in Christ that allows him to ignore the obstacles of contradiction, pain, denial and death; an impetus that is irresistible because the Father guides him through the night and receives him as the final dawning at the end of night. And so, through his act of total obedience, Jesus is released into total freedom, and the absolutely boundless space of God and of death, of everlasting night and everlasting death, lies open for his effective action. From the beginning he need not "care" (about the functions of living—"what you shall eat or what you shall drink, about your body, what you shall put on", Matt. 6. 25), for Jesus' lack of anxiety is a submission which leaves everything for all time in the hands of the Father.

Who is a Christian?

Clearly, the dogma is, in both its basic principles (Incarnation and Trinity), also the quintessence of the Christian way of life: doctrine and life must stand or fall together. Jesus Christ is not only the eternal Son of the Father who in his life and suffering shows us and gives us the Father's mercy: he is also a genuine human being who provides the initial impetus for the Christian life. He gives us the "space" in which to live a life of faith, but he does it by making himself the first and model act of faith. Although God can be apprehended and known in a thousand fragmentary ways throughout the whole space of his creation, there's still only one way in which he can appear substantially (though still in a certain mysterious obscurity): in the unlimited consent of his creature—a surrender in spirit, a declaration of readiness to go as far as God wishes, to be required and used as much as God might find necessary, and through self-denial to provide as much "space" for the will of God as God might wish to lay claim to.

We pray for all this to happen, every day, as Christ told us to: "Hallowed be thy name"; but for the most part we do it with an inadequate understanding of the implications of the words. "Thy name" means that by which man apprehends the distinctive appearance of God in the world—what reveals his unique reality as the only true, almighty, living God among us; those deeds which only God can do and through which he has made a "name" among us. All this ought to be "hallowed"—ought to be experienced and acknowledged as holy and divine. We pray that the reality of God will move the spirit that is within us; be felt and realized in us—despite all our resistance; and stay in us to predominate over all impulses contrary to God.

We pray "Thy kingdom come". God's kingdom is God himself to the extent that he is recognized as the only Lord. God as he really is and not as we'd like to think of him. The space where our own conceptions hold sway is still our own kingdom. God's kingdom is God with his own power and not our human forces which we pretend to use on behalf of God—only to replace his will with our own. Nothing can obscure God's power more and prevent his kingdom from coming more than emphasizing our own authority in order to establish the kingdom of God that is to come.

We pray "Thy will be done on earth as it is in heaven". As in heaven where you are, so on earth where we are. If your will fills heaven—the "place" where you are, where your name is hallowed and your kingdom has come —may it also fill the earth where we are and which we govern, where your name is still hardly known and your kingdom still hardly visible. Our earth has its own laws which you have enclosed in it and given us in trust to discover and develop. May your heavenly will be known and incorporated in those laws which are earthly and not heavenly, created and not divine; and may this happen through our co-operation in administering the earth not in the spirit and impulse of the earth but, ultimately, of heaven.

That's what we're really praying for; and if we don't want to babble away more fruitlessly than any pagan we shall remember that we are creatures of God, that there's a clear distinction between heaven and earth in the words we say. Then we shall accept in a spirit of Christian hope the clear promise that, if we give him room to do it in, God's will can be done not only with God in his heaven, but among us on earth.

COVENANT AND CONSENT

All this shows how precarious it is to apply the word "covenant" to the relationship between man and God. They don't make the sort of agreement in which each sets his conditions and one of the partners settles for a position halfway between them—splits the difference, as it were. In this particular covenant of union, you don't have—as in other cases—two equally entitled partners facing one another on the same level. This is so little the case that the description of man as a "partner of God" is, theologically, conspicuously lacking in taste (i.e., Mary as a "partner" of the Holy Spirit!). What seems to be a contractual agreement actually relies entirely on a unilateral choice by God. This choice (which becomes visible in the case of Abraham) results in a promise and an undertaking that means, as far as man is concerned, that he is justified in trusting in God's mercy towards him; that he can accept, believe and base his life on the truth of this grace. On Sinai this personal choice becomes a collective choice to which the nation is asked to give its consent. Free choice by God is an act of grace which extends the permission freely to accept the state of being chosen and God's indwelling in the nation—yet another indication of the unity of freedom and obedience.

This free answer to God is realized in Mary's acceptance as a "daughter of Sion" of the fulfilment of the covenant: God's becoming man. Her acceptance fulfils the event that took place on Sinai and serves as a model for Christian life in the Church of the future. It also fulfils the first three petitions of the *Our Father*—requests that are fully heard by God because the form of the covenant has been provided in full. Mary's consent is unconditional and therefore indissoluble : it opens the way to the final, irreversible devotion of God to the world, beyond which nothing "more" ultimate can be expected on God's part. The weakness of the consent given in the Old Testament forced God to add clauses—stipulations and threats—to his covenant : he alone will not be unfaithful, but Israel will be and therefore has a terrible expiation to make for its betrayal of the Ever-faithful who cannot break faith with his covenant. We might say that, at that time, the ultimately valid Yes of God included a parenthetical No. But the "Son of God, Jesus Christ, whom we preached among you . . . was not Yes and No; but in him it is always Yes, for all the promises of God find their Yes in him" (2 Cor. 1. 19-20). This visible Yes which God gives to the world with Christ and his saving death enters into the Yes of the "handmaid of the Lord"—an affirmation that is hardly audible to the world yet indissoluble. This Yes is the basis and essence of the Church of the New Testament. Any man who genuinely echoes this Yes in his own life is a living member of the people of God; and the more comprehensive his affirmation, the more he is "of" the Church.

The consent of the people of God which we hear in the acceptance made by Sion, Mary and the Church is entirely brought about and made possible not only through God's promise of grace, but through the fulfilment of grace in Jesus Christ, God and man. He alone is the indissoluble unity of the divine Yes to men and of the human Yes to God. Therefore he is the continuance of the covenant— the ever-continuing new and eternal covenant. He *is* the covenant because his humanity is lived in complete obedience to his divinity : in order to proclaim God, and until the last to use himself and allow himself to be consumed in this mission. He is both priest and sacrifice.

Who is a Christian?

The Yes of Christ and his mother-bride-Mary-Church is absolute because it is freed of all conscious or unconscious restrictive conditions; and the Christian life of the Christian is measured against this absolute Yes. This acceptance is the form of Christianity—the form which can be put on only by the man who wishes to enclose his life in it. It is an absolute form and impatient of all conditions. It asks everything and makes excessive demands of the sinner—who always sets conditions. It allows the man who has said Yes faithfully to discover, humbly though inexorably and perhaps brutally (or possibly the cross isn't brutal?), the unexpected consequences of his agreement. For he hasn't said Yes to a predictable plan of his own, but to the plan of God who is always greater than man and whose ways of doing things always seem different to man's expectations. This experience of the Other will prove decisive: it will show whether his Yes was spoken to God or to himself, whether it was faithful obedience or personal speculation, whether God's kingdom or the kingdom of men is to come.

Therefore the actual tribunal which divides the sheep from the goats, revealing faith and the lack of faith, is the cross. Jesus promises Peter the cross with the words: ". . . another will gird you and carry you where you do not wish to go" (John 21. 18). The prophet Agabus foretells Paul's forthcoming suffering by taking the apostle's girdle and binding his own hands and feet, saying: "Thus says the Holy Spirit, 'So shall the Jews at Jerusalem bind the man who owns this girdle and deliver him into the hands of the Gentiles'" (Acts 21. 10-11).

This decisive expansion of the human will, which up to now was anxiously concerned with self-preservation, to adjust to the size of the unrestricted and unpredictable will of God, doesn't occur as the result of human action but through the imposition of suffering. As long as man disposes there's no experiential evidence that he is obedient to God. Obedience to suffering is the demonstration of obedience to God. Nothing can replace this experience of and entry into the fullness of God. Christ himself "learned obedience through what he suffered" (Heb. 5. 8).

In man, therefore, there is an essential distinction between knowing and learning—particularly with regard to faith. The concept of "trial" (of man by God) is basic to Scripture. God himself is only "sure of" a man when he's tested him—like gold in the fire. "Count it all joy, my brethren, when you meet various trials" (James 1. 2).

IT GOES FURTHER THAN YOU THINK

And so Christianity proposes something very unusual— unusual when you set it against the general longing of all religions for union with God. Unless they express themselves in purely ritualistic forms, other religions can't go very far when they come to the question of abrogating the distinctions between God and the world, or allowing man to approach the reality of God (in death, ecstasy or absorption, and so on). Christianity asks how this union between God and man is possible when each is essentially different and remains so. But it provides the answer: union is possible since God gives his love the form of obedience, and man gives his obedience the meaning that is love. This happens if he agrees to be taken by God (whom he loves, because God has loved him) beyond everything that he himself can plan, condone, desire and endure through his own power. This passing beyond every thing that is peculiar to man takes him into the area of divine freedom.

Transcendence is not essentially "eros" (which is only the desire to pass beyond); it is faithful obedience through the strength of God who commands. Just as Peter strides over the waves because he is supported by the power of obedience; just as Lazarus stands up and walks, no longer a corpse because transformed by the power of obedience.

The word that calls us out beyond the sphere of our own designs and finite desires has to be hard on us. It must be if it's to crack open the hard shell of our finite being and explode the pillbox of sin we shelter in. That's why all the Lord's words reported in the gospels are like hard-tempered steel. Until the end of the world human beings will break their teeth on Jesus' words. But in the kernel within this steely exterior, the Lord's words hold infinite sweetness. They are inexorable in nature and similar to those of the Old Testament—but this serves only to emphasize the actual, free and supreme nature of the living God whose holy will remains infinitely superior to all human striving, longing and understanding and which, in so far as man is a sinner, is opposed to them. Human desire and longing (*voluntas ut natura, eros desiderium*) can never be the *final* standard of moral behaviour when God has made known his free and loving will. Because it is directed towards the unconditional, man's desire can prove a major criterion for what is to be prohibited or (in self-conquest) sought after in this finite world; but it will be of use only up to the limits of man's own understanding. If a man wants to set himself the highest and most exacting moral ideal to follow, it will have to be an ideal that he himself can trace out and justify and therefore appreciate as just and adequate. It's neither possible nor justifiable for man to wish solely of himself to go beyond the limits of such an ideal. It's not possible because the created will, being free, touches on the absolute (it wouldn't be free otherwise) and contains its own justification for striving for the absolute. But it's essentially impossible for the human will fully to conceive of the absolute as love which is free in itself and extended to him. What the absolute means as love only the God of love can make clear to man beyond all human criteria of human desire and longing.

That is why the primary form of decisive love by the human creature is obedience and not a state of already knowing (with God in the rear) what love exactly is and how it declares itself: in selfless concern for the poor and needy, shall we say. But: "you always have the poor with you, but you will not always have me" (Matt. 26. 11). However judicious they may seem, before all such programmes designed by human beings there is the underived fact that eternal love exists of itself. Whereas all earthly programmes divide their substance for distribution ("Why was this ointment not sold for three hundred denarii and given to the poor?" John 12. 5), all expenditure must go in advance and without any calculation to everlasting love alone, and for the sake of that love in itself ("Let her alone; why do you trouble her? She has done a beautiful thing to me . . . She has done what she could; she has anointed my body beforehand for burying": Mark 14. 6-8).

The unrestricted Yes of Mary of Bethany is the finished "work", the exhausted "wealth" of man; but it's infinitely more meaningful, weighty and fruitful than all programmes designed by men themselves. It is greater because the man who loves in this way doesn't calculate exactly the extent of his own ability, but dedicates his attempt to love to the love of God, for free disposal of the love that is God. And God will use it for his own purposes—which man does not foresee and the revelation of which (now or on the last day) will astonish him because it will be the greatest possible happiness. The "blind" love of Mary is used by God for his purposes in the passion of Jesus. Without knowing exactly what she's doing, she anoints the Lord for his saving death; and so, in the name of the loving Church, she stands for the agreement of mankind to this work of God's merciful grace. As a "handmaid" she is, like Mary the mother of Jesus, incorporated in God's work. Nothing more purposeful can happen to a man.

The "work" that Jesus praises here is the absolute work for which Christ can offer no equally effective substitute. It's not a charismatic strength of faith that can move mountains; not spiritual or angelic eloquence, which without love is just empty chatter; not the high seriousness of prophetic theology; not magnanimous concern for the poor ("If I give away all I have . . ."); not even martyrdom (or the celibate life, or witnessing to God; for despite all these things, if he hasn't got love man is nothing and gains nothing (1 Cor. 13. 1-3). All excessive demands men make on themselves in order to plan good works and carry out the best possible proposals for human happiness fail in the promised greatness: what God demands is the surrender of the heart in faithful love.

But it's impossible for man to make a fully serious surrender to God without sharing in the sorrow of the Mount of Olives. There's a decisive point on the way of the Christian life where human nature has to accompany Christ into death. Its mature growth must be cut down; its understanding must enter the darkness of night; its cultivated self-perception must suffer the harshness of discord. Steel must strike against steel. If the sinner weren't hardened by sin, God wouldn't have to be hard with

70

him. Even the least hardened of hearts—that of Jesus (or Mary)—must be tempered for representation's sake.

No wonder all of us always try to escape this moment; no wonder Christendom postpones, represses and finally forgets it. The history of the Church can also be depicted as the history of all the substitute offers it makes to God in order to escape the real act of faith. And so we're back in the realm of equivocation, where things that are very good in themselves can be the expression of a secret flight from God. There's another way to see the whole cultural drive of Christians who build splendid cathedrals, empires, poems and symphonies to hold the content of their faith; the entire system of a "closed government" of the Church which, in its legalistic ethic and casuistics, offers protection and security and a place of decisive appeal opposed to the exposures and risks of faith. Nowadays of course it's taking the opposite course : the abdication and relativization of this authority in view of the emancipation of the so-called "mature laity"; this, together with many other symptoms, could also be a sign of fear and flight.

A MESSAGE OF COMFORT ONLY FOR THE POOR[8]

Both the Old and New Testaments are full of beatifications of the poor and warnings and threats issued to the rich. The poor are those who because they lack possessions are free to receive God and his message. Mary has chosen the "good portion" because she makes her whole soul empty in order to keep it free for the one thing that is "needful" —the arrival of God's word. Martha on the other hand does too much because she is "rich" in herself by planning how she is to receive and entertain the Lord.

The word of God always comes at a moment inconvenient for the rich, because it claims all the available space already occupied by their own possessions. And so the message isn't a happy one for them; instead it's painful and perhaps even a judgment. The first Mary recalls a major pronouncement of the Old Testament when she sings: "He has put down the mighty from their thrones, and exalted those of low degree; he has filled the hungry with good things, and the rich he has sent empty away." Already Anna, Samuel's mother, had sung: "He raises up the poor from the dust; he lifts the needy from the ash heap" (1 Sam. 2. 8; repeated in Ps. 113. 7). Judith says something very similar: '. . . thou art God of the lowly, helper of the oppressed, upholder of the weak, protector of the forlorn, saviour of those without hope" (Jud. 9. 11), Because of their poverty and powerlessness, the poor or humbled (the same word: *anawim*) are despised as well as oppressed. Through the mouths the prophets God demands physical as well as spiritual justice for them (Amos 2. 6; Is. 3. 15; 10. 2; and so on). But they will obtain this justice only in Christ who begins his ministry with a blessing on the poor in spirit, who are also those who have been emptied (*katharoi*, "pure"), who cannot by themselves find redress in justice and are reviled, persecuted and have all kinds of evil uttered falsely against them (Matt. 5. 3-12) for the sake of Christ and the kingdom of God. All the promises of God are valid for them, for they have nothing else to expect. In the parables they are shown as having time to follow the call, whereas the rich are wholly tied up in their own cares. Because they have nothing, they think nothing of themselves. They are always in debt to God and can stay behind in the temple with the publican, recognize their guilt and return home justified.

God's poor are those who are always "immature" before God; whereas the "mature" and knowing are the rich, the pharisees and scribes. But God promises that "on that day . . . I will remove from your midst your proudly exultant ones . . . For I will leave in the midst of you a people humble and lowly. They shall seek refuge in the name of the Lord, those who are left in Israel" (Zeph. 3. 11-13). Those who are poor and usually designated as humbled, despised and ignored—insignificant nonentities —Christ proclaims to be the "little ones" or "children", the "lowly" or "last". In the world there are insignificant and meaningless people about whom there's nothing very much to say—they just don't seem to count in the ordinary way. But they are like the Christian Corinthians to whom St Paul says: ". . . not many of you were wise according to worldly standards, not many were powerful, not many were of noble birth" but "God chose what is foolish in the world . . . what is weak in the world . . . even things that are not, to bring to nothing things that are" (1 Cor. 1. 26-28).

It's not difficult to see that in this emphasis on spiritual poverty Christ also implies actual "literal" poverty, which he sets as an initial condition for his disciples and took as his own lifelong rule. Only if there's actual poverty in the first place is it possible to hope that the rich (in material and spiritual goods) will learn some conception of what poverty "in spirit" means. Of course it's possible even that the publican possesses more worldly goods than the pharisee. But if we don't begin with material poverty, all our talk about spiritual poverty is high-flown talk and nothing at all comes of it. Then every pharisee who gives tithes of all that he gets (Luke 18. 12) and every publican who gives the half of his goods to the poor (Luke 19. 8) might think he was already poor in spirit. It's a different matter with the poor widow who gives all she has to those who are even poorer and thus provides the same *tabula rasa* as the disciples actually picked out by Christ.

In the Old and at the beginning of the New Testament physical barrenness is emphasized just as clearly as total poverty. The inability to get a child, bear it and bring it into the world brings considerable humiliation on a woman: she is simultaneously despised and pitied. She can never bring to fruition what even an animal is capable of. She is not fulfilled as a human being and disappoints both her husband and her family. Very close to this biblical sterility (usually a prerequisite of God's promissory activity—as with Isaac, Jacob, Samson, Samuel and John the Baptist) is the misery and contemptibility of virginity for the sake of God, because God, true to his promise, will bring about fulfilment in no other way. Hence Mary describes herself as the *humilis ancilla*, the handmaid of low estate whom the Lord has looked down on from above (Luke 1. 48). The grace of fruitfulness for God is the extreme paradox, just as in Isaiah the daughter of Sion calls out at the sight of her sons: "Who has borne me these? I was bereaved and barren, exiled and put away, but who has brought up these? Behold, I was left alone; whence then have these come?" (Isa. 49. 21; recalled by St Paul in Gal. 4. 27).

Here we have the heart of revelation, which is good news and brings comfort only to the poor. It bears fruit only in the unfruitful, as they can "possess the land" in God, will "receive a hundredfold and inherit eternal life" (Isa. 57. 13; Matt. 19. 29; etc.) only in the obedience that is faith and allows them to be led beyond all attachment to self. Only in this way does the receptive earthly kingdom of man "correspond" to the seed which God sows: it does not bear fruit that through careless hearing and forgetting of the word soon withers away; but it persists in a *habitual act of faith* which is known in the tradition of the Church as the *act of contemplation*. This is the attitude of a thoroughly open and receptive soul that persists in the hearing of the word. Thus Mary "kept all these things, pondering them [meditating] in her heart" (Luke 2. 19, 51). Thus Mary of Bethany persists in the purely contemplative reception of the word and so does the one thing that is needful.

THE PRIMACY OF FAITHFUL CONTEMPLATION

Therefore the contemplative life is essential and central to the life of the Church as a whole. For the Christian there can be no external action without inner contemplation (which is the existential dimension of faith), since it is quite possible to fulfil his life by inner contemplation without external action. The contemplative act is the permanently basic act of all external action: it is active and effective, fruitful and missionary beyond all external undertakings of the Church.

The Church bears witness to poverty in the bad sense if it no longer understands the meaning of poverty; if, with increasing boldness, its theologians opine that contemplation (to which the Church has since the third century given serious support in an external form also) is a foreign body, the laborious and finally victorious excision of which has taken nearly two thousand years. Thus Cardinal Suenens speaks in his book *The Nun in the World: Religious and the Apostolate* of "stages of development" by which the enclosure of nuns (something he clearly deplores) is at last to be modified and ultimately almost completely suppressed. Angela Merici, Pierre Fourier, Francis de Sales, and Vincent de Paul are stages "of a battle fought for the liberty of the Spirit. St Vincent de Paul established a beach-head but he did not conquer the whole terrain" (p. 42). For Cardinal Suenens, in general, this victory would be the freedom and boldness of external employment in the service of our human brothers. According to him this work was the initial impulse in each case of the foundation of the major orders of the past. The later nervous withdrawals into cloister and enclosed cell were partial betrayals of the initial intentions. The fate of the order founded by Mme de Chantal can serve as an example. Suenens certainly recognizes (but only as an extreme exception) a life of pure contemplation of the kind sought by the first hermits and cenobites. This life was "seeking God principally in himself and for himself. It corresponds to the duty of direct adoration and is centred on the liturgical life—*Opus Dei*—and on the virtue of religion. The apostolic life, on the other hand, is oriented towards God in himself and the service of God in serving one's neighbour . . . the apostle abandons God for God's sake" (p. 45).

Here we have a conception of contemplation that is correct neither theologically nor historically, and which Suenens subsequently though only partially corrects (where he describes the inseparability of a life lived exclusively for God and being at the disposal of the Church). When talking about contemplative faith from a Christian viewpoint it is not permissible to imply the validity of the Greek philosophical concept that accepts an unequivocal unilateral "ascent" from the temporal to the eternal, away from the world to God. This concept appears in an attenuated form not only in Syrian and Egyptian monasticism (Evagrius and his school) but also in St Thomas Aquinas; but it can be connected with the apostolic direction to the world only superficially and belatedly.

Contemplation has to be conceived of biblically; then it includes the total answer of the faithful man to God's word: which is unconditional devotion to this word and to its purpose of world redemption. This was the way in which Anthony, the Father of the monastic life, fought his highly active representative battles against the spirit of evil. Thus Origen firmly emphasized the rôle of the contemplatives as similar to that of Moses who lifted up his arms to heaven during the battle and, despite his position on the mountain, in this way fought alongside the people of God as they struggled below. Thus Teresa reformed the Carmelites in order by prayer and total sacrifice to provide the Church with power to replace the losses of the Reformation. Thus the other Teresa conceived of her contemplation even more exclusively as the centre of the Church's missionary work—and, in obvious conformation of this, the Church declared her general patron of the missions. Thus Charles de Foucauld knelt daily before the tabernacle in the desert, knowing that he could not help the world more deeply in any other way.

The attempt to console the "old style" cloistered nuns by saying that today they as well as the growing number of secular institutes have their justification in the Church because they "all bear visible witness" (*témoignage*), has truth in it, but not the whole truth. The decisive efficacy of genuine contemplation—to the dismay of all statisticians —is to be found entirely in the realm of the invisible. Faith is given to God without reckoning or consideration of the cost, and what God does with it does not ultimately concern those who are faithful. The faithful are called on and exploited to such an extent that the way of contemplation, followed honourably and unswervingly, usually passes into darkness: into a state in which nothing is seen any longer, a state which has been prayed for and for which renunciations have been made, a state of no longer knowing whether God still listens, still wants the sacrifice, still receives it. . . .

It's devoutly to be wished that the Church won't sell its deepest mysteries and highest privileges for the mess of pottage of external apostolic satisfactions; that it won't abandon for the sake of psychological, sociological and statistical considerations the ultimate risks that can be justified only on theological grounds. This would be an indication of the kind of levelling down process I described at the beginning of this essay. The voice of the Holy Spirit is not heard when the message of Thérèse of Lisieux, Edith Stein and Charles de Foucauld is thrown to the wind. The witness that would be abandoned then is not primarily a witnessing to the exclusively contemplative form of life, which will always remain the affair of a few people with a special vocation; it is a witness for the contemplative foundation of every Christian life, as I have tried to show.

Any one who's not prepared to listen to God in the first place has nothing to say to the world. Like so many priests and laymen today he will meddle in and concern himself with a great number of things, to the point where his awareness is deadened and he's completely exhausted. In doing this he misses the one needful thing and yet will even falsify in order to justify his omission. Nowadays you can hear priests and laymen everywhere spouting vindication of their vast concerns—enough self-justification to make any straightforward person shudder. The age of contemplation, they say, is finally past. Contemplation really belongs to a cultural epoch that has gone for ever (here we spy the ghost of the Greek philosophical concept of *Theoria*) in which it was considered high-minded and noble—and reserved for the nobility, too, who had the leisure for it—to gaze at the stars and experience a longing for the absolute. Any romantic who happens to stare up at the sky these days runs a fair chance of seeing nothing but serried ranks of factory chimneys and an atmosphere full of exhaust gases. We live in a sober workaday world to which the whole man is irremediably yoked. In the modern block of flats and the individual apartment with its interconnecting rooms packed with noisy kids, there's no free space for individual concentration and private devotion. As for the city priest who can't seem to get a moment to himself, day or night : if he manages to snatch a few minutes for the essential part of his daily office, well, that's certainly the most you can expect from him. Nowadays the place to meet God is in the midst of action— otherwise you'll miss him. The engine's really started this time. The world's on the move and no one's going to let it idle again.

That's a fair summary of the way they talk, and they don't bother about contradictory opinions. They've come to terms with things as they actually are. They're so assured in what they do that they even think their abandonment has something tough and realistic—even heroic —about it. *"Dieu premier servy"*, said Joan of Arc. Yes : if God is served first, then our whole secular life can be interpreted as the service of God; our slave labour in the factory of mankind can be an act of free dedication and acceptance; our continually inexpedient encounter with the world as it is can be supported by and joined with a meeting with God which persists and is present all the more clearly to us, the more emphatically we make it the very foundation of our life of faith. Then the basic decision "Thy will be done" (just where it thwarts me and makes demands on me I hadn't dreamed of) is carried out in everything that makes any claim on us. In this sense secular life and its activity become the practice of contemplation. Now God's not in the rear; instead we're going towards him in open expectation of meeting him.

We can only proceed towards God if beyond all our own problems we keep room free in us for his will—for the demands of his will. If all our programmes, forecasts and calculations are set in motion and kept going by the call of God, which is always greater than man's conception of it, we shall be on our way to God. Only in such a condition of absolutely decisive obedience before all else, can the Christian describe his life and activity as love. Otherwise his attitude and devotion wouldn't exceed those of any average human commitment to the world—which experience shows us often achieves much more and is much more prepared for greater sacrifices than the commitment of some Christians.

THE MEANING OF ONCE FOR ALL

And this is where the holding back from true commitment so frequently met with among young Christians today is questionable. They want to commit themselves but at the same time they tighten their grip on the controls. They want to commit themselves fully, but only for a foreseeable period. If they signed themselves on for longer than that they wouldn't be able to check whether the commitment was still worthwhile; after all, they want to remain free to think things over and use their abilities in another way if they feel like it, or make new contracts. They're sure that this kind of procedure will allow them to increase their total output and stay in charge of their own destiny. They'll always do what they find comprehensible—as long as it seems worthwhile.

It's rather like a "companionate" or "temporary" marriage. After all, there's such a thing today as the "temporary religious life": but they're both self-contradictory. The first is experimental sex. The second can't be more than a tranquil breathing space for very busy people (as circumstances permit) in some abbey that puts you up for a short time. But just as a marriage is formally entered into by a mutual contract for ever; just as you can become a priest only for ever, and not temporarily; so the nature of things is echoed in the actual form of agreement determined by the appropriate authorities. In each case what matters is an ultimate stress on God in a Christian life and all its individual actions.

This ultimate part is intimately connected with Christian obedience in faith. In all three cases—the states of marriage, priesthood, religious life—the purpose of existence is irretrievably surrendered to God. We throw the ball up into the air in the hope that God's hand will catch it. But if a man is prepared to give up only part of his life, then even the authorities make reservations . . . there's no foundation to the promise. Perhaps a man is going to the missions for three years as a lay assistant and when the three years are up—well, we'll see. Or a girl becomes a nursing sister but makes the reservation that she might get married after all. Things change so quickly today.

But all genuine fulfilment of an individual life comes

from the commitment that's made once for all. Kierke-
gaard called the other kind of commitment the "aesthetic"
existence (which he thought found its clearest expression
in Don Juan); but this real kind of commitment he called
the "ethical" (as marriage) and the "religious" (as denial
of marriage). A bad thing if the aesthetic life is chosen on
ethical pretexts. But it's the order of the day for a
good word to be misused in a dubious context—"mature"
in the phrase "mature Christian", for example.

WHAT IS A MATURE CHRISTIAN?

What does the word mean in biblical revelation? For
example, are there any mature Jews in the Old Testament?
Did Christ, obedient to the Father unto death, become
mature? In the case of the Church, can we describe a priest
or a member of a religious order as mature? Or is the
word applicable only to the laity? Perhaps they're mature
when they grow out of the immaturity of clerical tutelage.
We'll have to open the Bible if we're to be at all exact
about this.

"Immature" (*nēpios*) can mean simply the normal child
("When I was a child, I spoke like a child, I thought like
a child, I reasoned like a child", 1 Cor. 13. 11.). "Out of the
mouth of babes and sucklings thou hast brought perfect
praise", Matt. 21. 16=Ps. 8. 1). But if the condition of spiritual childhood extends beyond the appropriate time, it's
reprehensible. Just look at Heb. 5. 11-12: "About this we
have much to say which is hard to explain, since you have
become dull of hearing. For though by this time you ought
to be teachers, you need someone to teach you again the
first principles of God's word. You need milk, not solid
food." Here immaturity is a lack of understanding, which

again comes from deafness to the word of God. The passage is about listening— ". . . you have become dull of hearing".

A similar passage is 1 Cor. 3. 1f. Before, Paul had said that the worldly man does not understand the Spirit of God; that to do that one must be a spiritual man; and that he, Paul, has the Spirit. Then he continues: "But I, brethren, could not address you as spiritual men, but as men of the flesh, as babes in Christ. I fed you with milk, not solid food." A reading of the whole letter in a attempt to grasp what St Paul means by the gifts of the Spirit of God which only spiritual men understand shows clearly that the essential answer is (in 1 Cor. 1. 18-2. 5): the "word of the cross" which is folly to the world but a folly which makes foolish the wisdom of the world. The immaturity of the Corinthians is that they haven't become aware of this "scandal" which alone ensures insight into the "spiritual truths" of God. This is more strongly underlined at the most important point (Gal. 4. 1-7), which is also the most paradoxical).

In the Old Testament the faithful are placed under the law as if under a strict task-master; but now, through faith in Jesus Christ, they are all children of God. St Paul expands a legal metaphor to explain this: "I mean that the heir, as long as he is a child, is no better than a slave, though he is the owner of all the estate; but he is under guardians and trustees until the date set by the father. So with us; when we were children, we were slaves to the elemental spirits of the universe. But when the time had fully come, God sent forth his Son, born of woman, born under the law, to redeem those who were under the law, so that we might receive adoption as sons. And because you are sons, God has sent the Spirit of his Son into our hearts, crying 'Abba! Father'. So through God you are no longer a slave but a son, and if a son then an heir."

Here the immature man is no longer the unripe Christian but the man who was faithful before the coming of Christ: the Jews were immature because they served God only by means of the law—"an elemental spirit of the universe" (administered by "angels", i.e., cosmic forces), and not in freedom and directly before God.

The release to genuine maturity as a son of God occurs through the Son of God, but in a strange way—so that the Son, submitting to the physical laws of birth into the world ("born of a woman"), is still under the law; whereas through the Spirit of this Son the slaves are made sons and heirs of God. This is the Spirit of long-suffering, submissive, unselfish, obedient love, as St Paul emphasizes (Gal. 5-6). It is the Spirit of those "who belong to Christ Jesus" and who "have crucified the flesh with its passions and desires" (5. 24).

Common to both these passages is the concept of the complementary nature of maturity and the cross. This is the meaning of the final sentences of the chapter of the Letter to the Hebrews already cited: ". . . everyone who lives on milk is unskilled in the word of righteousness, for he is a child. But solid food is for the mature, for those who have their faculties trained by practice to distinguish good from evil" (Heb. 5. 13-14). God's "word of righteousness", which was manifested in Christ, is the same as the "word of the cross" or, in the Letter to the Hebrews, the word of the high-priesthood of Christ. But this still seems tasteless and indigestible to immature Christians: they need mature senses in order to appreciate and digest it. Only those enlightened in this way "have tasted the heavenly gift", "have tasted the goodness of the word of God and the powers of the age to come" (Heb. 6. 4-5), because the existential truth of the death and resurrection of Christ has prevailed in their lives and become the criterion for distinguishing good from evil.

If this mature appreciation of the nature of the cross has been cultivated in an individual and in a community, the apostle can consider his wet-nursing at an end. "For a good purpose it is always good to be made much of", he says to the Galatians, "and not only when I am present with you. My little children, with whom I am again in travail until Christ be formed in you!" (Gal. 4. 18-19). This "form" that must appear in the Christian is the same one that the Church originally impressed in him through sacramental baptism in the hope that it would become the ultimate form of his refractory material: "Do you not know that all of us who have been baptized into Christ Jesus were baptized into his death? We were buried therefore with him by baptism into death, so that as Christ was raised from the dead by the glory of the Father, we too might walk in newness of life. For if we have been united with him in a death like his, we shall certainly be united with him in a resurrection like his. We know that our old self was crucified with him . . . we believe that we shall also live with him" (Rom. 6. 3-8). Therefore the man is mature who fulfils the objective sacramental reality subjectively and existentially—in himself. He no longer needs continually new outside compulsions to be crucified to the world. Freely and independently, once and for all, he has "crucified the flesh with its passions and desires" and can say with the apostle: by Christ "the world has been crucified to me, and I to the world . . . I bear on my body the marks of Jesus" (Gal. 6. 14-17).

Finally, if we look for an example of maturity which

would also serve as a standard for everyone, it's worth meditating on Acts 16. 6-7: "And they went through the region of Phrygia and Galatia, having been forbidden by the Holy Spirit to speak the word in Asia. And when they had come opposite Mysia, they attempted to go into Bithynia, but the Spirit of Jesus did not allow them." Paul and his companions made plans—undoubtedly in a spirit of Christian selflessness and with the intention of doing what was best for the kingdom of God—but the Holy Spirit had other, really far-sighted plans. One plan against another.

The Christian who is prayerfully united with the ever present, ever guiding, ever commanding Holy Spirit of Jesus and is able to understand that he must give up all that he has planned himself—for the sake of God's plan—is a mature Christian. He willingly becomes material in which the form of Christ is impressed. Such "material" is raised from its "passivity" to the highest form of activity as the "matrix" and "mother" of Jesus (". . . is my brother, and sister, and mother", Matt. 12. 50).

THE MISSION GIVES LIFE

Christian maturity, therefore, is not so simple and straightforward a matter as most people might think. It's never just a question of forming one's own conscience according to certain allegedly Christian principles. The conscience is part of our human nature and so it's certainly the basis of our natural moral activity; but in so far as we are Christians, our conscience must always listen for and remain open to the Holy Spirit of Christ which, free and unrestricted, rules in and over us. The Spirit won't let himself be put down in bottles and principles to be neatly corked and sealed for all time. Only the fresh and living

power of a continual readiness to listen offers any opportunity of hearing and understanding the Spirit. This presupposes an extreme docility and a fully prepared and
supernaturally instinctive obedience—the opposite of
what we so crudely think of as "maturity". The more
obedient we are to the free Spirit of Christ, the more
mature and free we really are. Anything else is self-
deception.

The conditions for entering this state of mind have
been mentioned. In utter seriousness we have to accept
the crucifixion of Jesus as the basic form of our earthly
life: only then will the "powers of the age to come" be
evident to us in the "goodness of the word of God". These
powers are the eternal, undying forces by virtue of whose
superiority the Christian has to distinguish, administer and
master earthly things. Of course these "powers" aren't our
own, but are made ready for us. We can "put them on"
like clothes, or like a new body that we can enter and
identify ourselves with. This is what the Bible calls "putting on Christ", "putting on the new nature" (Rom. 13.
14; Gal. 3. 27; Eph. 4. 24; Col. 3. 10). This is the way to
Christian freedom and maturity.

But as long as we are on earth, this freedom is charac-
terized by service. We haven't given ourselves this new
free nature: we owe it to the grace of God in Christ.
Previously we were slaves to sin, but now we "have become slaves of God", and the return for our services is
"sanctification and its end, eternal life" (Rom. 6. 22). This
life of freedom in the service of God is a life of vocation.
In order to be offered it, we have to offer ourselves to it
for ever. Sacramentally, the finality of this service is baptism and its irremovable sign; but baptism requires existential ratification. God offers no "temporary" appoint-

ments or commissions. "Permanent appointment" to the service of God is the basis for continually requiring the servant to take on tasks that are always new and unexpected. He's always on duty : "Lord, what wilt thou have me to do?" (Acts 9. 6 : Vulg.).

Ultimately no servant of God can justifiably think that he has fully understood his mission and that in order to carry it out there are no more questions to be asked, that it's all right now to cut off communication with the Lord's will. The powers which give him life are not the powers of the present age, but those of the "age to come"; he himself is an "eschatological being" for his new nature relies wholly upon the acts of faith (in Christ), hope (in what is still unattainable), and love (directed away from himself to God and his neighbour). The eternal motion of this threefold act keeps the servant always on the point of departure for, and always on the point of return to God.

But the Christian is also a Christian only as a member of the Church. Baptism is an act of the Church and allows entry into the physical community of the Church. No one becomes a Christian off his own bat. And the Holy Spirit who makes a man mature if he wants to be, is first and foremost the Spirit of the Church. The Church is the holy body of Christ and his immaculate bride.

The Church doesn't mean just the clergy any more than it means a sort of club that anyone can join for a small subscription. The spirit of the Church is the spirit of holiness : of Mary, of the apostles, of the saints who are its supports—whom the Lord will make pillars "in the temple of my God" (Rev. 3. 12). A Christian who is not prepared and trying as hard as possible to make this his spirit is immature. "Educators" remind him of this. He is provided with means and practices to develop him, to heighten the external condition and transform it into an inward one. As long as he remains opposed to this spirit—a stranger to it—the devotions of the Church will seem strange and legalistic to him, and he will complain about formalism and ritualism. But he has only his own immaturity to blame for such impressions. If he decides once and for all to align himself with the Spirit of the Church he will become a mature Christian. And if he takes on full responsibility he can no longer afford his former enmity, opposition, carping and fault-finding.[9]

Because the individual Christian is a member of the Church and Spirit and life come to him from the whole Christ as Head and body of the Church, his Christian vocation is always an ecclesiastical "charisma"—a call to service out of grace. St Paul describes the distribution of the ecclesiastical graces to the members of the Church through the Holy Spirit according to the needs of the entire organism as the "measure of faith" or the use of gifts in "proportion to our faith" (Rom. 12. 3-6). The "measure" of the task allotted me, seen from a Christian viewpoint, is not up to me : I have to accept it as a pre-ordained quantity. This is the basic "ecclesiastical obedience" of the member of the Church; it is deeper and more basic than the obedience of the layman to the cleric, in so far as the latter relationship implies an external hierarchical function and an official "court of appeal" to ensure that doctrine and sacraments are retained and transmitted in a pure form. The relation of the member of the Church to the apportionment of the task is (as shown in revelation) so objective and at the same time so spiritually alive a relationship, that its specific realization in a charismatic and official relationship of obedience to a "superior" (according to the so-called evangelical "counsel" of obedience) is quite Christian.[10] Hence the apostles who gave up everything for Christ's sake obeyed him as a man who for them was the specific realization of God's will, and did this long before they understood that this man was the Son of God in the full sense. Hence, too, St Paul requires from his churches (for example, in his second Letter to the Corinthians) an obedience which, in its sudden and drastic demands, in the extent and intensity of the activity asked for, far exceeds the merely official and hierarchical function of the average cleric. It would be wrong to say that the tone of St Paul's requests for obedience shows that the young Church of Corinth is basically immature. In full consciousness of his appointment by God's Spirit (I cor. 7. 40), St Paul isn't reticent about using mock superiority ("boldness") as a form of spiritual therapy for the immature (who give themselves away by pseudo-mature self-assertion): "I beg of you that when I am present I may not have to show boldness with such confidence as I count on showing against some who suspect us of acting in worldly fashion . . . for the weapons of our warfare are not worldly but have divine power to destroy strongholds. We destroy arguments and every proud obstacle to the knowledge of God, and take every thought captive to obey Christ, being ready to punish every disobedience, when your obedience is complete" (2 Cor. 10. 2-6). Only then, when he's sure of their obedience—St Paul is saying—will the Church have achieved the maturity that will open its eyes to the legitimacy and accuracy of his reprimand.

A Christian who does not understand the unity of maturity and Christian obedience within the Church is far from being mature. Because the connections between the two are clear only to the really faithful pray-er, and without this prerequisite everything is lost in shallow and dangerous chatter, the concept of maturity has to be used sparingly and carefully. Most of those who continually trot the word out clearly fail to understand the meaning given to it in the Bible. They talk—with God in the rear—about things (*"vox temporis vox Dei"*) that are allegedly demanded by present circumstances and the structure of contemporary man. But they don't ask what Christ demands. They lay down the terms for their mission themselves. They think they know how the kingdom of God can best be served, and so they don't hesitate to mutilate those parts of revelation that are really most essential to life yet don't suit their own conception of modernity. This process is known as demythologization.

LOVE: THE FORM OF THE CHRISTIAN LIFE

But my readers will be impatient. How can I go on talking about Christians for so long without mentioning the main commandment of love for God and our neighbour? I've talked a lot about it—and talked intensively, but in such a way that the emphasis was on the particular by which this love was to be distinguished from the general, already known, love that is humanism. The essential point—the one that brings us to a sudden halt—is to be found in St John's sentence: "In this is love, *not* that *we* loved God *but* that *he* loved us and sent his Son to be the expiation for our sins" (1 John 4. 10). This stopping short and then starting out again is the main thing from the Christian viewpoint. It's an essential preliminary to our own love.

The direction of travel of this love passes from us towards God and our neighbour: both are inwardly joined in Jesus Christ, God and Man. God with all of us, and Man for all of us. "If any one says, 'I love God', and hates his brother, he is a liar" (1 John 4. 20). "He who does not love remains in death. Any one who hates his brother is a murderer" (1 John 3. 14-15). "He who does not love does not know God; for God is love" (1 John 4. 8). The nature of our love is determined by our receiving it from God and correspondingly extending it to our brothers.

"By this we know love, that he laid down his life for us; and we ought to lay down our lives for the brethren" (1 John 3. 16). "Beloved, if God so loved us, we ought to love one another" (1 John 4. 11). This movement of love which comes to us from God and goes from us to the brethren has its focal point in our own thankful love of Christ, who gives us love as his commandment: therefore it is his first of all and only subsequently ours: "If you love me, you will keep my commandments. . . . He who does not love me does not keep my words. . . . This is my commandment, that you love one another as I have loved you. Greater love has no man than this, that a man lay down his life for his friends. You are my friends if you do what I command you" (John 14. 15-24; 12-14).

Clearly the special nature of this love is that it imitates the example of Christ and persists until death. The general law of sympathy that exists in the cosmos is a neat and judicious equilibrium between self-preservation and self-sacrifice. This helps to preserve the species: biologically, when parents sacrifice themselves for their children's sake; sociologically, when soldiers die for their country. But it would be madness if anyone said he wanted to lay down his life for everyone. Nevertheless, Christian love brings in this very moment of eternity when God's self-sacrifice enters into love. God has given himself wholly up to death for the sake of every man; and on the cross every man finds release from his sins out of the inconceivable bounty of

God. This reality of God's sacrifice is behind every man. Everyone is what he is—the beloved of the eternal God— in spite of any opinion I might hold of him, any way in which I might see him. Faith lends me the eyesight to see behind every man the love of God's Son; and perhaps I can see that love all the more clearly, the more God's Son had to suffer for him. The poorest of all are the closest brethren of Jesus Christ; and the poorest of all are not only those who have to undergo physical deprivation. They are just as much the spiritually poor who have no window through which love can shine in the darkness of their self-centredness, pride and avarice. It's heresy for a Christian to say that the Son of God didn't die for all sinners. There is no one who would have stood at a greater distance than any other from Jesus on the cross. Every man stood as close as possible to him: to the point of transformation, of identity. Every man was his neighbour. This everlasting and inconceivable quality entered love on the cross.

To "lay down his life for his friends" doesn't mean that one can die bodily for every one. Only the Lord can do that. But it does mean that we must be basically ready, in case of serious need, to give or hold back for anyone's sake: ". . . if any one forces you to go one mile, go with him two miles" (Matt. 5. 41)—or three or as many as might be necessary. And St Paul says: "To have lawsuits with one another is defeat for you. Why not rather suffer wrong? Why not rather be defrauded? (1 Cor. 6. 7). And finally, where eternal salvation comes in question, where it could come to the question of him or me: "For I could wish that I myself were accursed and cut off from Christ for the sake of my brethren" (Rom. 9. 3).

It is astonishing (and humiliating) that in order to

explain the teaching of love for one's neighbour Christ chooses as his example a "heretic": the Samaritan. What the priest and levite omitted, this man did—beyond the confines of enmity between Jews and Samaritans. Whether he did it out of sympathy or mere humanity, the Lord raises his intentions into the light of his own love. He counts his deed as Christian love. And Christ himself, God's Son, puts himself in the ordinary and anonymous ranks of those who have loved. Who can know precisely where in the wide world such a surrender of an individual's own life is taking place? Or where one man sets his neighbour above himself? It rests in the hidden depths of God.

For the Christian this neighbour who is always before him becomes the glass in which he can see the light of Christ. The other man seems faceless, a chip broken off from the universal mass, a cell in the same shapeless whole of which I myself am part. But if the encounter becomes a real meeting, this nonentity becomes a face in the crowd —another person behind whom lies the freedom, dignity and uniqueness of the Quite-other. Christ gives him a face, unlimited importance and superiority; and Christ presses me out of my own anonymity. I must stand up with this other man, recognize my own features in his countenance, be responsible for myself and for him. Out of the indecisive dream world of a moment ago a new clarity is born. Perhaps there will be resistance, but here is reality, here is my own level: I've found it at last.

Behind my brother is God's commitment unto death, and for God my human brother actually has eternal value. As I look into my brother's face I look into the depths of the inconceivable. As I look, all aspects of revelation emerge, clearly delineated, real. They're no longer dry phrases, passages and verses in meaningless isolation: now they are necessary colours with which the painting is made complete. If Christ were not God, then his sacrifice wouldn't be exceptional and its fruit wouldn't be present to us. If he were not man, that mysterious representation could not take place that allows me to address my brother. If God were not threefold, Christ couldn't have done his work out of love for the eternal Father, God wouldn't be love in himself—or in order to love he would need the creation, and then wouldn't be God any longer. And if there were no grace of faithful obedience, this present encounter couldn't take place adequately in the reality of Christ, for I could cherish no eternal hope for this brother of mine who stands before me. If Christ weren't present in the Sacrament, we wouldn't be joined to him in this indescribable way in which we seem knit together like parts of one body, in "remembrance" of him. If there weren't any acknowledgement of sin then we'd stay locked up in ourselves for good without any humanly reasonable act to change us from lost to found sons. And then that distance between my brother and me would be restored, and we couldn't remove it; then over both us the high divine Judge would hold sway, and neither of us might anticipate his judgment.

But the distance between us is mysteriously mediated by an irremovable figure: by the woman who was mother to the child who does not forget her loving intercession and authority; by the woman who bears us all in her womb and for whom we always remain her children whom she has borne in pain and carries for so long a time, until the travails of the Church are at an end and the woman rejoices and "no longer remembers the anguish, for joy that a child is born into the world" (John 16. 21).

No limb of the body of Christian faith remains motionless when it meets its neighbour. All these members of the body are asleep, lifeless and theoretical, between the covers of a catechism; but they all stretch and strain to move effectively when they meet one another, when, in this encounter, theory becomes practice. A practical Christian is a man who undergoes this resurrection of truth in the reality of his life. When this happens the practical Christian becomes a practising Christian. And a practising Christian is one who loves Jesus and "keeps his commandments". Practising means putting these commandments into practice, and we know that all the commandments of Christ are embodied in the one commandment of love. We shall be justified by this commandment alone: according to the practice in our lives of practical, active love—or our lack of practice. This unique commandment is also the standard for finding out whether we know God: "He who does not love does not know God; for God is love" (1 John 4. 8). There is no such thing as theoretical faith, or being a Christian "in theory". Christianity is a form that can't exist without the matter just as the form of a piece of sculpture can't be actual apart from the stone, wood or metal that takes that form. The matter is where love manifests itself, where it shines; the matter is the object of love's self-sacrifice: the neighbour who can only be so close to us because God in Christ is present in him. My neighbour can be loved so much only because in him there appears the everlasting love of God for me and for him; the love which is the First and Last of all things, and of our encounter as well.

But, the reader will say—this description of Christian practice doesn't seem to include what we usually think of when we talk about a "practising Christian". But it does.

God Before Us, or: Who is a Christian?

WHAT DOES "PRACTISING" MEAN?

It means execution, carrying out, putting into action a pro-
fessional or some other kind of ability. A doctor practises,
for example. He uses his skill for the sake of his patient.
A Christian practises by using the graces given to him for
the sake of his fellow man. Therefore it's not quite
enough, if you want to decide whether a man is a practising Christian, merely to ask if he goes to church every
Sunday and receives Holy Communion at Easter. For one
thing, that's a minimum demanded by the commandments
of the Church; for another, it isn't the main part since the
living of Christian love is most important. Perhaps these
externals are more accurately seen as symptoms of a
man's attachment to the Christian life. Of course we have
to ask if they're healthy or unfavourable symptoms. They
would be the latter if the man thought of Christianity as
an insurance company offering policies due to mature in
heaven, and paid the minimum permissible premium. But
they would be the former if he were aware that in order
to last, his Christian life needed this regular activity of
self-discipline which, in the long run, is no negligible
sacrifice. For example, listening Sunday after Sunday to a
sermon which makes your teeth grate with annoyance.
There's considerable significant value in this kind of sacrifice. To some extent it can justify the almost exclusive
stress and attention on this particular form by a priest
who's got used to it as a meter for calculating the number
of sheep in his flock.

But the words "practising Christian" are still misused
if applied to one—certainly not unimportant—individual
aspect of the whole activity.

The Church is the light of the world, the salt of the

D   97

earth, and the leaven in the dough. Therefore it is relative to the world, just as the sun is fire concentrated in order to give effective light and heat right up to the limits of the solar system. You can't do much with yeast and salt on their own. But if you put them in, under or on meat or dough, and mix them in, they prove their value and fulfil their nature. The Church is the concentration which is absolutely indispensable for the desired expansion. But "If salt has lost its taste, how shall its saltness be restored?" Concentration means attentive and active consideration of the essential.

"Practising" means going to church on Sunday. In the gospel and epistle at Mass we hear the word (and if what we hear then really isn't enough for us we're obliged to add to it by reading the Bible ourselves). Of course this hearing isn't done for its own sake, but implies our own activity—our own conversion so that when we're outside we can faithfully direct others to God. The Eucharist is the realization of Christ in the midst of the community and the congregation, and in the midst of every heart. It welds all hearts into one body, for no one is alone in his commitment but always has the whole community there to back him up. The Eucharist occupies the very centre of our hearts so that I am not alive, but "Christ in me". Paradoxically, in the most personal devotion and thanksgiving, it is the emptying of the self for occupation by that which is greater than self: Christ and his own, the Church and the world. And so the dual celebration—of word and sacrament—necessarily ends with the commission: *Ite, missa (missio) est.* The man who has reached "maturity" through this celebration is sent out. He has heard the word from the cross and seen the body on the cross: he has received them. They are one; and so he has made them the form his life will take in the world, for the world.

The second part of "practising" is the activity of confession: once or more often in the year. This is an extremely personal act and in no way a mechanical process. To the extent that we respond to it—through the sincerity of our acknowledgement of guilt, the genuineness of our sorrow and resolution to do what should be done—we become certain and even aware of the deep-reaching effects of the grace of forgiveness. Our model is the prodigal son.

We have to realize and recognize the full extent of the lack of gratitude that we show in the vegetation of our everyday life while one Man must pay in death and abandonment for our forgetting God. We have to become aware of the full extent of the frightful distance between our own rule of life and Christ's rule of life—to love God and our neighbour as ourselves, or, more deeply, our neighbour and ourselves in the Spirit of Christ. All the other commandments handed down from Sinai and all the laws of nature make room for this Christian light that shines out as the right standard for self-judgment. If this standard is once discovered in a genuine examination of conscience for confession, it must be applied, realized and "practised" in our everyday lives. Penance is also to be thought of as the light and salt of our entire life; and the light is not to be hidden under a bushel. Penance doesn't shut us up in an air- and sound-proof confessional. It's an act in the Church; and it's very significant that in the earliest years of Christianity a confession was made openly, in front of the congregation. We are egotists who have driven ourselves to the limits of the Church's love or even quite out of its fold; therefore penance should reconcile us not only with God but also with the "communion of saints". It should give back to us the spiritual cleanliness that enables us to be representatives in the world of the Spirit of Christ and of this holy community of saints, which is our Christian duty. We know very well that absolution is a grace and not something we have deserved; that we shouldn't parade ourselves—like pharisees—as "converted" before the unconverted; and that our attempt to lead a Christian life should point out the way to the only source of all grace and vocation.

"Practising" also includes life in the temporal framework and rhythm established by the Church—the "Church year". The cyclic commemoration of the most important events of our salvation ought to become an exercise in the Christian way of life. The Christian should celebrate the feast days in a practical way, just as the "present moment" of Christmas, Passion, Resurrection and Pentecost recurs in a very practical way for the Church as the holy bride of Christ. We seem to have got so used to this rhythm that we can't appreciate the joy and wonder in it any longer. But what if we banished the feasts of Christendom? How stale and insipid the flow of time would be. For to practise Christmas means to carry the spirit of Christmas into our lives: it means that God, though rich, became poor for our sake, in order to enrich us with his poverty (2 Cor. 8. 9). This feast has been scandalously misused and turned into the birthday of Mammon; it's been packaged, tinselled and labelled until it's its own opposite. The Christian must take it back to its original meaning.

Similarly, the contemporary softening of the bones must not be allowed to affect the season of penance before the day on which Jesus died; and Easter should be the feast of our resurrection, not to a merry holiday in this world or optimism about the evolution of the cosmos, but to the Father of Jesus Christ who has taken him up for us and with us through the power of "his glorious grace" from everlasting darkness into eternal life. Just so, the Ascension is not the Lord's goodbye to us, but his raising us up to "sit with him in the heavenly places in Christ Jesus" (Eph. 2. 6); and the gift of the Spirit at Pentecost is the starting point of the apostolic mission to the "whole world", ". . . in weakness . . . not in plausible words of [human] wisdom, but in demonstration of the Spirit and [his] power" (1 Cor. 2. 3-4)—and, symbolically, the long weeks after Pentecost leave us all the time we need for that.

Finally, the individual Christian will practise his faith not just by following the social and pre-determined paths of the Church's year, but equally by making his way along the unordained and unknown paths of his own destiny. He'll certainly recognize as much on days of rejoicing, but the acknowledgement will be even more effective on days of trial. Then he will be put to the real test and required to direct his life towards God in a practical way. Then he will come up against his limitations, feel his weakness and experience unlimited disappointment and disillusionment with himself and his life. Someone he loved is dead; someone has let him down in a really rotten way: a chill wind blows through his emptiness. He has to make a decision: it's God or nothingness. And there are even more effective humiliations which the Lord has promised his followers as a great grace and which, if they come, must always remind us of him: "A disciple is not above his teacher, nor a servant above his master; it is enough for the disciple to be like his teacher, and the servant like his master" (Matt. 10. 24). They are signs that the Lord and Master has not forgotten his servant. Failures, setbacks, slights, calumnies, contempt, and finally—the quintessence of life—a major bankruptcy: all this was the daily bread of Jesus Christ and will always be the fate of the Church in this world. The man who wants to belong to the Church has to look forward to things like these. And no possible twist of "evolution" will change it in any way.

"Practising" therefore is central to the whole context of the Christian life. Undoubtedly it's an act of recollection and concentration ("Do this in remembrance of me"), but always undertaken with the purpose of expansion into the world. We must discover God in the effective signs of his word and his sacrament, but only in order to seek him more vehemently and passionately (*ut inventus quaeretur immensus est*) where as yet he is not, and where we must bring him; or rather (since he already is everywhere), where he is already hidden and waiting for us to find him.

IV

Dispossession and the Universal Mission

HOW DOES A CHRISTIAN SERVE THE WORLD—AND NOT
SERVE IT?

WE have considered the essence of the Christian life and
should have formed a positive attitude to what I previously
called the fourfold trend. This seemed a rather doubtful set
of tendencies because it set its sights a good way from the
focal point of true Christianity, taking for granted that
enough was known about that already. Instead the movement seemed to be an attempt to achieve as much as
possible *on the periphery*: often in a way that revealed
a desire to ignore the centre as much as possible and substitute something peripheral as a new mid-point.

But the word of God is inescapable. It says what it says
so clearly that it can always be picked out from the inadequate emollient some people use to soften it. You just
can't force the Bible to say that the Christian is primarily
a servant of world evolution and only in that way a
servant of Jesus Christ (i.e., of the cosmic Christ who will
come eschatologically on Omega day). Twist the texts how
you will, you'll never wring one drop of evolution out of
them. So all that's left (unless they want to write off the
whole revelation as the product of cultural immaturity[11])
is the attempt to *insert* Holy Writ as a moment in a com-

prehensive cosmic philosophy. Since this philosophy is graced with the title of theology (see above), and since the innocent reader understands theology as Christian theology, the deception seems to work: biblical theology enters and disappears into a cosmic philosophy (= natural theology) as a moment of that philosophy, only to be resurrected as the eschatological point of the philosophical system and turned into a Christian Q.E.D. Of course it's done by using the image of the glorious cosmic Christ, but ". . . in that case the stumbling block of the cross has been removed" (Gal. 5. 11). Now everything becomes easy and cosy. The Christian who, until now, was so ridiculously stubborn, at last climbs down and collaborates. He's applauded and congratulated for his progressive attitude, and received with honour into the company of those who are seriously concerned about the future of the cosmos.

It's precisely this facility that must be suspect to everyone who has considered the prospect Christ outlined for his disciples. Suspect too is the synthesis which includes the supreme word of God as one of its mere observable moments. The synthesis is managed in such a way that Christian teaching is accepted to the extent that it's a "positive ethic", but abandoned when it resists this metamorphosis.[12] This means that man has corrected the word of God and replaced the unacceptable bits from his own storehouse of knowledge. The process can be seen (provisionally) as an end-product of the disastrous history of Christian gnosticism, which repeatedly changes faith into knowledge, revelation into philosophy, and the search for truth into a discovery of truth; which has served to discredit Christianity more basically than some other things. Contemporary atheism is to a considerable degree the justifiable reaction against this kind of Christian "being in the know" and knowing too much: from the Christian view-point the two together are neglect of God.[13] Christian gnosticism corrupts philosophy as much as theology. It philosophizes biblical revelation by setting the regulative and redemptive word of God in an observable system; but it also theologizes philosophy by paralyzing the open ven-ture of universal and human history in optimistically pre-dicting its course. The kingdom of this world and the king-dom of God—nature and grace—retain their true dignity only if they preserve their own legitimacy and the free-dom of application proper to them. The convergence of both realms (on a certain "Omega point") is an impossible interpretation as long as God retains his freedom to come like a thief in the night and to keep the power of the cross in his own charge.

There's another kind of synthesis forbidden to the Christian. I have called it "integralism"; in fact, it's no more than the practical application of the gnosis already described: in other words, it's the recruiting (oblivious of God) of specific secular forces for the alleged extension of the kingdom of God on earth. The intention may be genuine, but the unacceptable part is the naïve presupposi-tion of the identity of the kingdom of God with a political, cultural or ecclesiastical influence, which is then practic-ally equated with the effective power of a group of Chris-tian Mamelukes who thirst after world conquest.[14] But we're not in the Middle Ages and the time is past for naïve equations of heaven with earth. All forms of Christian "freemasonry" will eventually make themselves suspect to and hated by Christians and non-Christians alike. Any-one who is party to such undertakings hasn't really con-sidered the weakness of the cross (which he's supposed to proclaim), the supreme power of God (which he wants to assist with earthly power), or the ways of earthly power (which he applies so innocently and uncritically).

We Christians are in a much more open and unprotected position than we'd like to be in if it were up to us alone. We are radically exposed: as Christians before the world and, through Christ, in the world. We should like to make the Church into a protective shield against the world, and our worldly mission into a shield against Christ's word and demands on us. But Christ disowns the worldly sword of Peter the integralist: he takes the part of the others and heals Malchus' ear. And the same night the world disowns the collaborationist advances of the same Peter, and puts him in his place: "Certainly you are also one of them, for your accent betrays you" (Matt. 26. 73). The anxious attempts to cover up are unmasked on both sides. The Christian is left exposed, where he must stand "in the whole armour of God", with only the "shield of Faith", the "helmet of salvation" and the "sword of the Spirit, which is the word of God", together with "all prayer and supplication" as his covering and weapons. He must also gird his "loins with truth", put on the "breastplate of righteousness" and the sandals of the "gospel of peace". All this is the total armour (*panoplia*) of the Christian which makes him "strong in the Lord and in the strength of his might" and gives him adequate equipment "against the principalities, against the powers, against the world rulers of this present darkness" (Eph. 6. 10-18). Or as the Lord says to Paul harassed by the messenger of Satan: "My grace is sufficient for you, for my [God's] power is made perfect in weakness [the weakness of man]" (2 Cor. 12. 9).

This means that in his exposed position—and *only* there —the Christian receives from God the assurance of every heavenly protection and weapon. If he runs away from his visible unprotectedness and takes cover elsewhere, the protection of God is lost. His exposure can mean "weaknesses, insults, hardships, persecutions, and calamities" (2 Cor. 12. 10) for the sake of Christ. All this is intentional —a sign by which he can recognize the state where he has no need to be afraid. Let the pendulum stroke of the speech of commission in Matthew 10 take effect: "Behold, I send you out as sheep in the midst of wolves; so be wise . . . and innocent . . . Beware of men, for they will deliver you up to councils and flog you . . . do not be anxious how you are to speak or what you are to say; for what you are to say will be given you . . . the Spirit of your Father [will speak] through you . . . you will be hated by all for my name's sake . . . it is enough for the disciple to be like his teacher . . . have no fear of them . . . what you hear whispered, proclaim upon the house-tops. And do not fear those who kill the body but cannot kill the soul. . . . Do not think that I have come to bring peace on earth . . . I have come to set a man against his father, and a daughter against her mother . . . he who does not take his cross and follow me is not worthy of me. He who finds his life will lose it, and he who loses his life for my sake will find it."

Peace is to be found only in the midst of the struggle between God and the world. Only when the Christian surrenders his own power does God's supreme power save him. Or, as we recognized earlier: God's riches are given only to the truly and actually poor.

But is this intermediate state endurable? Is it possible to live like this for any length of time? Doesn't it produce a kind of schizophrenic consciousness, trying to unite two kinds of personalities? Isn't it eventually to the disadvantage of both kingdoms? Isn't an attempt to escape into one realm or the other all that can normally be expected of a man placed in this condition of theoretical difficulty (*aporia*)?

ONE COMMITMENT IN SPITE OF EVERYTHING

Before we give a decisive answer, we mustn't forget that the natural man, in so far as he is a spirit, already transcends the closed world and finds his 'normal' location (as every religion and philosophy of the nations of the past recognized) between relative and absolute, between the world and God. If humanity today forgets this quite elementary truth—or tries to ignore it for the sake of a "secular presence in the world", there's a regression in human wisdom—and the world is the poorer for it. The injunction "Be true to the world!" can only concern a thoughtless and reckless exploitation of earth and world and survey it from above as the "lord of creation". The thoughtless and reckless exploitation of earth and world we experience in our technological age is a very dubious way of remaining true to the world. But these are just preliminary remarks, for it's the Christian we're in search of.

Yes, let's consider the Christian. In him the general tension between nature and spirit is clearly increased. He is radically "uprooted" from "nature"—indeed from the "world" altogether. Yet, for this very reason, he is all the more radically sent back into the world as a whole. On the one hand he is in the world though not of the world. On the other hand, he is told to go out to all the world, which means right in and not just "to". The pendulum doesn't stay fixed in the centre: it moves right out.

Earlier we looked for and found an apparently impossible point of unity between the unique activity of God made man and our subsequent activity. This point was the Yes given to God as an indication of absolute readiness to serve—the Yes of loving obedience. Surely it ought to be possible to find a corresponding point where our mission as human beings in the world and as Christians (in and with the Church) can be identical? It must be possible if in his revelation God takes his own creature seriously, not destroying it but fulfilling it in all advances, stresses and despite all apparently excessive demands. The answer in both cases must come from the same point of moral consciousness (otherwise no answer would be possible). The unique point has to be the same point we've already isolated: the Yes of commitment to God.

It's not difficult to discern this unity. The Christian says Yes to God and God gives him his mission to mankind. The human being in the world says Yes to his material tasks in the world, in his family, State, and the organization he works for: in each case, he is a useful member of the whole to the extent that he's a servant of the whole. In both areas there's a pre-condition of his "usability": namely, that the Christian or fellow human has freely and responsibly identified himself with his work. This making of an act of willingness to serve includes a renunciation of egotism.

For the Christian this act must be radical and thoroughgoing; otherwise he wouldn't be a genuine believer. For the human being in the service of the world it *can* be radical as well: when he wants to see his life as undivided service to the whole, and the little he can contribute to the whole expresses his unstinting readiness to serve. But with many the sacrifice is partial. For example, they work only in order to earn and in the intervals lead an egotistic life of pure consumption. Or in their relationships with women (in or outside marriage) they seek mainly their own pleasure, whether they acknowledge it or not, think it's normal or not. There's no need to stress that the selflessness of the faithful as of the moral man is by no means self-forfeiture, self-dissipation or flight from self (a process which certainly does happen and which Max Scheler analyses and censures in his study of the nature and forms of "sympathy"); that both have as pre-requisites the calmness and secrecy of self-possession and, for the believer—prayer. The rhythmic movement between concentration and expansion finds its sense of direction in devotion: the man who loves must be a deep spring if he's to draw for others from his own depths.

Because Christ is the deepest, most inexhaustible and unfailing of all springs and the faithful Christian has this original as a model to follow, there can be no reason for the opposition of personal devotion as a Christian to personal devotion as a member of the human race. Selflessness —being at the disposal of another—presupposes in both areas that a man has something to offer, that he is efficient and knowledgeable in the secular realm, and that as a result he will contribute to his missionary activity the interest and application that are critical for its particular efficacy. Selflessness presupposes too that he is happy in his calling, whether it is prestigious as in the case of a research scientist, or insignificant as in the case of mechanical work in a factory which could possibly be taken over and even done with greater speed by a machine. But to the extent that and as long as it is a service, it requires the accurate performance expected of a conscientious workman. The servant in the parable is "faithful in a very little" and as a reward is given "authority over ten cities". The majority of people have to carry out their work in life as if they were minute wheels in a gigantic prefabricated machine where those that drop out can easily be replaced with spares that run just as smoothly.

But every man who serves is a unique man, for his loving heart cannot be replaced. He contributes his personal love to the great anonymous whole of love; this kind of self-surrender, when conscious, is almost like death. A sacrificial death. And you can't blame the poor man for leaving his place vacant once in a while for pleasure and recreation. You can't blame him for cherishing the hope and almost the certainty that the world as a whole is moving towards a meaningful future; that the minute wave that was him, long ago made part of a nameless river, will come to rest eventually in some unforeseeable ocean. The secular man can't know more than this—unless he doesn't really subscribe to this kind of naïve concept of the future, and some faint understanding of the truth leads him to explain his life and pour it out as a sacrificial gift.

Whether he in fact does this need not concern us here. What is critically important is that it can be done by the Christian in the secular realm and that such effort is already exerted in the objective direction of human existence (although, as a spirit, man finally transcends finality). It is certain that the man gets the most out of his life who applies it as fully as possible to a task with a purpose which seems worth doing for that purpose. Without devotion to work there's no total commitment, and the reverse is true as well. Therefore the final abandonment can't be measured against mere performance. The part played in this performance by ambition—the will to power—is no longer decisive. There is a good sort of ambition: to carry out one's work as fully as possible and get the thing done. Not just Christian morality but natural morality already includes this concern to clarify motives and refine the subjective attitude into an objective concern with getting things done.

But perhaps the objection will be raised that the Christian isn't capable of this full application to worldly things because his head and heart are elsewhere ("For where your treasure is, there will your heart be also"): in the eternal life to come. Surely for him earthly life is only a passing moment, a momentary rest in an inn where it's not proper to dilly-dally, look around, rearrange things—let alone try to improve them. And this is certainly the reason why Christians are always to some extent preoccupied, not entirely taken up in the task, if it's a matter of constructing the future of the world. Still, it's only right to ask who constructed Western civilization if not Christians—almost exclusively. If they had no interest in worldly values how did they manage to construct the material images of the supernatural and eternal we owe to them? When you get down to it the servant in the Gospel is asked not to bury his talent, but to use it for profit. Surely this means that he's asked to obtain the fullest possible return from the insignificant cash value of his years on earth. Doesn't the Christian know better than other men the real value of this unique earthly existence—this plot of ground which conceals an everlasting treasure it's worth digging for and risking everything for? It's quite right to say: "Do not lay up for yourselves treasures on earth, where moth and rust consume and where thieves break in and steal" (Matt. 6. 19). For the man who wants to work and to give, without getting anything out of it himself, has his treasure in his devotion; and where his treasure is, there is his heart also. Christian teaching increases almost infinitely the possibility of his devoting his life to a task; not only the external performance is included in the sacrifice and its fulfilment—it also encloses the intention, the will, and above all the suffering when nothing active can any longer be done.

Christian hope doesn't imply disconnection from the world; it offers an infinite deepening and intensification of the individual's hazy optimism that his having existed for the whole has not been completely useless and meaningless. An ordinary man's desire is to have made some contribution to the building of the kingdom of humanity; the Christian's desire is to have contributed something small to the kingdom of God in the world and the realm of men. His hope cannot deceive: he hopes that what human time marks up as futile will not be thought valueless as an entry in the books of life and fruitfulness. Therefore in an age which thinks of progress as something visible, something that can be assisted only from a technical and mechanical viewpoint, the Christian becomes the guardian of a deeper concept of progress: he doesn't fall for the delusion that things are moving ahead only when the results can be measured in figures. But he'll have only a bitter account to give—a record of omission—if he's got nothing moving here when his urgent duty as a Christian was obvious yet other men did his work for him (if we're to put it in the vocabulary of materialism).

The Christian has always had to offer an example of self-dispossession. The Gospel begins with that very act. But now other people have taken over the administration of this activity, and plan things so that the dispossession is of necessity successful. The Christian should include himself in this process so that, as it proceeds, he can manage to preserve freedom (as far as it's still possible). Then it would be made clear to all men that there is only one true form of commitment: to one's brothers and to the world. For that is the commitment of God who gave his own Son for the sake of the world; the commitment of Christ, who can lay down his life and (with those he has raised up) take it up again; the commitment of Christians as they say Yes to the Lord; the commitment of the man to whom his brother is worth more than himself.

A LOWLY CHURCH

Now we can examine the real significance of the contemporary trend. The movement of the Church beyond its own boundaries to its Christian, Jewish and non-Christian brothers could be the movement of self-dispossession—the self-emptying—of God and Christ. It would certainly be so if Christians didn't try to alleviate their own condition or plead for diplomatic concessions on the pretext of others' needs, but instead were striving for the most difficult of all things: unprotected, selfless exposure. That's the task with an end in itself, whereas all others (for instance in the hierarchical discipline of the Church) are relative to it; they are good in so far as they assist the main work, but bad to the extent that they obscure it. The selfless Church seeks only the honour of its Lord and not its own glorification; for the Lord never sought his own honour but that of the Father. In the Bible it looks for the word that teaches it an increase of obedience. In its liturgy it seeks not the self-satisfaction of the congregation but the adoration of its Lord and investiture with his power so that it will be strong enough to pursue its vocation. In dialogue with the separated Christians it tries to fulfil the imperative commandment of its Master: unity as love. It seeks its mission in the secular world about it—its mission as the leaven that is effective only when it disappears.

In its present "breaking out" its intention is not self-justification but much more self-humility. It must look for a process of education in humility in all these new departures precisely because all these elementary things have occurred to it so astonishingly late in its life, and because it was oblivious not only to the Holy Spirit's urgent prompting but to the suggestions of an entire co-world of Protestants, Humanists and Communists. And in its initial, still hesitant dialogue with the Jews the Church must feel really humble—small, as they say. Why should the Jews bother to listen only to the voice of the Church after everything that has happened over a period of nearly two thousand years? Perhaps it's permissible to hope that the dissensions within Christendom could be settled to a considerable extent if there's sufficient genuine humility. But just think how the Church must appear to our Jewish brothers. What is to be done?

Perhaps the Church can submit an inclusive admission of guilt, beginning with a great list of its various examples of non-observance of Scripture: that God retains the right to judge others; that the Church is grafted on the holy tree of Israel (Christians should take very careful note of the fact that if God hasn't preserved the noble natural branches, the same could happen much more easily to the shoots taken from a wild tree and merely grafted on the cultivated one); finally, that all Israel will be saved since God's promises are irreversible. The vis-à-vis of Israel and the Church is based on the Bible itself; therefore it's not something within the discretion of the Church. The Church itself in a mysterious way exists dialectically to Israel: the dissension stems from the central point of salvation history and the precise nature of its redress is the concern of the Judge of all things. For the Church, however, this means that—in a way it can't ultimately fathom—it remains relative to Israel just as Israel is relative to the Church. And so the Church is not in itself purely and simply the whole—not purely and simply the kingdom of God. "So do not become proud, but stand in awe", as St Paul reminds the Church in this context (Rom. 11. 20).

At no point is the Church so seriously required to be humble and lowly as in this case. It's not out of place to say that it is asked to realize its shame and disgrace. We shouldn't try to shrug it off. It would only make things worse. After all, a Christian is always in disgrace—really humiliated—in confession. And such public sins—committed before the whole of human history—can't be rubbed out of the memory of history merely by acknowledging that they were sins. So let's stand up and take the blame: not virtuously but because it's deserved. And there's no possibility (as I said at the beginning) of individual Christians escaping the general censure—it's our Church. At this point it would be wise for Protestants who might be tempted to throw stones and still wish to be called Christians to remember that, in this case, the history of Christendom before the separation is just as much *their* history as it is ours: the Church didn't begin its existence in the sixteenth century.

When humbled and lowly, the Church must find the way more easily to those who are humiliated and despised —and those who have been neglected because it's hardly profitable to lay out an excessive amount when the desired improvements are so insignificant. Just as the mark of the earthly existence of Jesus Christ was selflessness, so it must be the mark of his Church on earth. The more earthly civilization organizes itself and undertakes campaigns against poverty, disease, hunger, illiteracy, the more Christians must take part in these schemes as human beings working with other human beings, and help them to progress. Governments and international organizations will steal an increasingly impressive march on the Church in terms of outwardly available means. Here too the Church is referred to the interstices between the well organized, profitable bodies; by joining those who are last, by taking the "last place" of the Gospel (Luke 14. 10) and becoming, like the apostles, "last of all" (1 Cor. 4. 9), the Church takes the place designed and reserved for it—the place that suits it. This doesn't mean that it should not try to extend, through its members and in as many non-Christian organizations as possible, its particular spirit of humble, uncalculating devotion (which, paradoxically, goes beyond the humanitarian spirit); it should do this right up to the highest duties and responsibilities of mankind. For these offices will be objectively and appropriately carried out precisely when the highest possible degree of selflessness makes real objectivity and detachment possible; just as we hope that the increasingly planetary horizon of man will influence the power struggles of particular groups, unions, parties and nations, by increasing the impartiality and therefore objectivity of their standpoints and arguments.

Although we seem to be able to see a definite evolution towards the universal in this secular domain, there's no possibility of evolution as far as the idea of the Church is concerned. Its idea and the essence of its being have already been given to it—when it was commissioned. At any time the Church can look back to its origin: in order to confirm and estimate its guilt in diverging from the ideal, and in order—from now on—to attend to and develop things it wasn't diligent enough to care about. What appears to be progress and development in the worldly sense would be a dubious form of activity for the Church. A record growth rate (in terms of figures), honour, riches, influential cultural and political gains can only cause the Church to feel uneasy, express its distaste and get the wind up in case God no longer remembers his people.

The position of the Church must remain paradoxical. It can be really effective only as a small flock, can only "leaven the whole lump" if it is concentrated leaven. Of course it's always open to the temptation of seeing this leavening of the whole as a sign of its effective activity. This is a temptation because in the last analysis the effectiveness of the Church can't be measured at all. Its most essential forces—prayer, suffering, faithful obedience, readiness (perhaps unexploited), humility—escape all statistical analysis. The correct approach is that of the organizations (*instituta saecularia*) which reject a direct (statistically measurable) apostolate in favour of a simple presence in the dechristianized world (*présence au monde*). Other organizations which use all possible means to strive after positions of secular and cultural power in order (so they allege) to help the Church, merely injure it and—not unjustifiably—make themselves and the Church odious in others' eyes.

Of course when we talk of the "Church", every Christian must realize that *he* is under discussion. The times are gone when the laity could shift their responsibility on to the clergy. The clergy are increasingly becoming the organization whose task it is to educate and maintain the people of God (*laos Theou*) in the true Christian spirit.

They have received their special graces of the priesthood, instruction and guidance for this very purpose. No layman today can begin a sentence with the plaint "The Church ought to . . ." without immediately asking himself if he is doing what the Church ought to do. In order to form such a sentence he has to make sure that by speaking in this way he really speaks in the Holy Spirit of the Church as the bride of Christ and communion of saints, rather than out of a private and uncharitable and therefore entirely unecclesiastical spirit of mere criticism. The Christian can't possibly start to ask and determine how far the Church is dispossessed and humbled without seeing that this salutary purpose is at work in his own life.

Finally, if we ask what arrangement of the various ways of life must be made so that everyone can see the essential nature of the Church is quite clear to everyone, the following order would seem appropriate: firstly, the "position" of those members of the people of God who have received and chosen the gifts of faithful obedience, poverty and fruitful "sterility" as the marks of their way of life; secondly, the people of God as a whole; and thirdly, its official servants (as *servi servorum*). But because this objectively correct hierarchy is always in danger of misinterpretation by sinful men as a hierarchy of honour, it's just as appropriate to reverse the proper order and, as usual, start with the clergy and put the complete way of true fulfilment at the end: especially since it's the due of those who choose to be last to be placed last.

PRAYER, HOPE AND PROFANITY

The Christian always has a lot more to learn about self-dispossession. Since he owes his freedom to Christ and thanks Christ for this, his self-emptying becomes prayer. And prayer, as long as man is a sinner and egotist, contains a leaden weight of reference to self. The pray-er is concerned with his salvation, with a "merciful God". He has every reason to beg for forgiveness for his trespasses, for strength in his weakness. And then he'll certainly pray for friends, acquaintances and relatives. And peripherally, when it occurs to him, he will pray for Christendom and the world. But as the Christian learns more about his way in Christ, his prayer will be emptied of self.

He prays for forgiveness of sins: here his own guilt is present to him, weighty and yet removed from him; for the thing to be feared now is that sin exists at all, whoever committed it. He prays for the coming of God's kingdom, the hallowing of his name, the doing of his will on earth. For the bread that God is to give to us all and primarily to those who hunger for it. Then for delivery from temptation and evil—especially of those who are almost hopelessly engulfed in darkness.

The more effectively the Christian learns to pray, the more his heart is emptied of self. He has a singular discovery to make. At first it alienates him—disturbs him almost to the point of intolerance. What he thinks of as his private silent room (where he thought to retire in extreme solitude to dwell with his God) has walls only to the world but none between it and heaven. Everyone in the triumphant Church can see in. The Book of Revelation tells us that everything that happens in heaven and on earth occurs as if in an immense public place. The prayers of the saints are visible to all, and taken up by angels to rise like incense before the throne of God. Nothing is private. The more intimate and personal an expression of love, the more public it is in the kingdom of God; the more everyone can lay claim to it. Not only the floor of heaven is made of transparent crystal, but all the walls too. Everyone has entry to the house in Nazareth, to the heart of the Virgin; even people with grubby shoes and ragged clothes for whose odour the last image you'd choose would be the scent of lilies.

Here Christians still have much to learn. Most of them are irremediably petty-bourgeois, prudish, affected and namby-pamby when it's a matter of personal piety. They must seriously consider if they're not well behind in the evolution of consciousness. Their existence, their heart, their prayer all form a single loaf of bread which everyone should share. Why shouldn't Christians take part in the Eucharistic mystery?[15] If they are members of Christ they should be at the disposal of their Head. They are in service and the extent of their service is a matter for the Master who makes use of them. They must recognize and acknowledge that they are wholly to be employed, applied and used. They must regulate the movements of their hearts according to their prayer. They must learn to pray the Our Father becomingly and appropriately: which means in the way Christ intends it to be prayed—not reducing the meaning of each petition by focusing it on themselves. There's no *I* in the Our Father: it's *we* all the way through. In this *we*, the *I* is abolished because transcended.

It's very hard to understand why, but once upon a time theologians held the view that each man could only hold out for himself the Christian hope in which there's no deception. But the opposite is true. Each man must hope for all his brothers, whereas for himself he can hardly avoid a moment of fear. Certainly it's true that complete love banishes fear, but who can justly claim that his

love is complete? But in meeting his brother he sees behind him the Son of man who died for him and who
intercedes for him with the Father (1 John 2. 1). He sees
him behind everyone—behind the whole world. And his
hope is nourished by this insight. He no longer hopes for
himself (to see God as soon as possible after his death)
while all the others have to wait in silence. True Christian
hope is eschatological and communitarian. It is part of the
longing of all creation for redemption. In this hope the
antithesis between the present and the hereafter is no
more. Some Fathers of the Church say that even the
blessed in heaven hope for the final and complete redemption of the world. This can be seen too from the petitions
in the Book of Revelation. The promise is made of a new
heaven and a new earth. The new heaven will be when
the earth is taken up into heaven. That will be the new
earth in which God's will is done on earth as it is in heaven.
Christian hope doesn't mean a running away from history,
but an advance along history—right to its end.

In this way the slogan "the secular world" of modern
"profanity" (secularism) is transformed into a truly Christian phrase. "Profane" means: outside the sanctuary
(*fanum*). For us the "pro" means that we're still not in it,
but also that we are always in front of it and advancing
towards it. The same is true of every meeting with another man: it occurs before the holy place—but it won't
happen in truth unless the Christian sees through the profanity that which is holy, and keeping his eyes on it,
advances towards it. In the process of moving forward
the difference between secular and sacred is cancelled. But
only in moving forward. The mordant discourses of the
transcendentalists on the total profanity of the world
deny the action of hope as much as the tipsy and exuber-

ant raving of the Teilhardists about the total sacredness of the cosmos.

The path of the slow movement of hope is illumined for the man who in faith and obedience has dispossessed himself. He takes the risk and makes his way along it without asking whether he's on foreign soil or in his homeland. When he senses he's in another country he knows that he's still on the way home and that his homeland will be none other than the foreign land, made new as the land of promise.

Notes

[1] Hans Jürgen Schultz, *Konversion zur Welt* (Furche Verlag, 1964).

[2] *Iphigenie in Aulis* (1788).

[3] *Iphigenie auf Tauris* (prose version begun 1778; play completed 1786).

[3a] The quotations from Pilippians are from J. B. Phillips, *The New Testament in Modern English* (London, Geoffrey Bles), © J. B. Phillips, 1960.

[4] Hans Eckehard Bahr, *Poiesis. Theologische Untersuchung der Kunst* (1961).

[5] Arnold Gehlen, "Das Engagement der Intellektuellen gegenüber dem Staat", *Merkur* (1964) 407.

[6] Walther Dirks, "Bittere Frucht", in *Das schmutzige Geschäft: Die Politik und die Verantwortung der Christen* (Walter-Verlag, 1964), p. 261.

[7] "When truth is—primarily or by deduction—predicated of several things, then it must be primarily predicated of that in which the full concept of truth is seen to be realized." St Thomas Aquinas, *De Veritate*, I. 2.

[8] I am indebted to Prof. P. D. Barthélemy, O.P., for this heading, which is taken from his penetrating analysis of the connection between poverty and the message of the Gospel.

[9] Henri de Lubac gives an excellent description of this transformation in his contribution "Credo Ecclesiam", in the *Festschrift* for Hugo Rahner (*Sentire Ecclesiam*, 1961, pp. 13-16).

[10] Cf. Willibrord Hillmann, "Perfectio Evangelica. Der klösterliche Gehorsam in biblisch-theologischer Sicht", *Wissenschaft und Weisheit*, 25 (1962) pp. 163-8.

[11] One theologian did not scruple to declare that it was part

of the kenosis or self-emptying of Christ that he became man so early on, in—from the evolutionary point of view—so immature an age. What a really brainy messiah we should have had today—only a couple of turns more in the evolutionary spiral of the contracting universe! Inconceivable!

[12] Cf. my article "Die Spiritualität Teilhards de Chardin" (a comment on the German edition of *Le Milieu Divin*), *Wort und Wahrheit*, 18 (1963) pp. 339-50.

[13] Cf. my article "Die Gottvergessenheit und die Christen", *Hochland*, 57 (1964) pp. 1-11.

[14] Cf. my article "Integralismus", *Wort und Wahrheit*, 18 (1963) pp. 737-44.

[15] "Because Jesus entire is pure in entirety, his entire flesh is food and his entire blood is drink. For every one of his works is holy and each of his words is true. And therefore his flesh is real food and his blood real drink. Secondly, Peter and Paul and all the apostles are real food, and thirdly, their disciples. And thus everyone, according in each case to his commitment or the purity of his intention, becomes real food for his neighbour. Every man has in himself a certain food. If it is good, and if he turns it to a good end, bringing forth goodness from the good stores within his heart, then he offers his neighbour real food." Origen, seventh homily on the Book of Leviticus.